D0687731

THE MYTH OF THE INFORMATION
REVOLUTION

302.2
T671

THE MYTH OF THE INFORMATION REVOLUTION

Social and Ethical Implications of Communication Technology

edited by
Michael Traber

SAGE Communications in Society Series
Series editor: Jeremy Tunstall
SAGE Publications
London · Beverly Hills and Newbury Park · New Delhi

LIBRARY ST. MARY'S COLLEGE
171008

Copyright © 1986 by
World Association for Christian Communication
First published 1986

All rights reserved. No part of this book may be reproduced or utilized in any form or
by any means, electronic or mechanical, including photocopying, recording, or by any
information storage and retrieval system, without permission in writing from the
Publishers.

SAGE Publications Ltd
28 Banner Street
London EC1Y 8QE

 SAGE Publications Inc
275 South Beverly Drive
Beverly Hills, California 90212
and 2111 West Hillcrest Drive
Newbury Park, California 91320

SAGE Publications India Pvt Ltd
C-236 Defence Colony
New Delhi 110 024

British Library Cataloguing in Publication Data

The Myth of the information revolution: social and
    ethical implications of communication
    technology. —(Communications in society)
    1. Communication 2. Technological innovations
    I. Traber, Michael   II. Series
    302.2   P91

ISBN 0-8039-8005-1

Library of Congress Catalog Card Number, 86-060437

Printed in Great Britain by
Antony Rowe Ltd, Chippenham, Wiltshire

Contents

Foreword

Seán MacBride

Many thinkers, particularly since World War II, have expressed the view that technological progress is running ahead of man's capacity to interpret its implications, and to direct it into the most desirable channels. The gap is disturbingly evident in such areas as biology, genetics, nuclear physics, cybernetics and, more recently, communication technologies. New technologies, advancing by their own momentum, often urged on by political pressure and economic requirements, impose themselves before they can be properly assessed or assimilated. Because of the speed of technological progress and of the concurrent breakdown in standards of public and private morality, the assimilation of new techniques eludes both ethical guidance and social control. Albert Schweitzer, the Nobel Peace Laureate, once pointed out that 'Man has lost the capacity to foresee and to forestall the consequences of his own actions.'

I would not like anything that I have said, or what others say in this volume, to be construed as advocating a slowing down in the use of technological developments. I would rather urge that, concurrently with the utilization of technology, there should be a constant assessment of the moral and social implications that will result from modern technology. This is an extremely important aspect of the 'micro-chip' revolution in which we are participating.

The use to which technology is put is seldom neutral. It is influenced by many political or financial considerations. It is therefore useful to know how decisions are taken concerning the main lines of emphasis that are given to innovations. It is also as well to know *who* decides research and development policies and priorities. It is clear that the general public exercises little or no control over such decisions. In the final analysis, it is not so much the consumers as the producers that decide what the market 'requires'. Technological developments demand careful scrutiny. Technical options may well increase the risk of manipulation, at both national and international levels.

The essays in this book deal with only one kind of technology, that of information and communication. Many consider this aspect the least lethal of all. Yet information technology is the lifeblood of many other technologies, and in fact is often the carrying mechanism through which other technological developments become operational. This book shows some of the implications which communication technologies are likely to have on the global economy, the distribution of political power, the growing gap between rich and poor and the relationship between multinational companies and national sovereign governments.

It is at this crucial stage of global development that Dr Hans W. Florin, in his capacity as General Secretary of the World Association for Christian Communication, gave the impetus and encouragement to search for moral values and ethical norms that might guide not only the churches but others ready to listen and think. This was no easy task, either for himself or for the global association of which he was chief executive for ten eventful years. He initiated new research. He created a number of international study groups. He was at the centre of a small movement of Christians who kept asking: communication for what, on whose terms, on what basis, with what principles and with what effects for the future?

It has been my privilege to collaborate with Dr Florin on the formulation of a new world information order based upon justice, democracy and dignity of all the people of this planet. Dr Florin has shown great vision in this challenging task, and I am delight·d that this book is dedicated to him.

I particularly appreciated Dr Florin's commitment to disarmament and the role that communication could play in the search for genuine peace. He once remarked to me: 'What a slow process this peace is! Our fears, prejudices, and greed make us shy away from peace rather than pursue it. As if it were easier to live with war on our own terms than with peace in which we, on every side, had to surrender our terms'.

If these words are the only ones quoted of Hans Florin in this book, they suffice to characterize a man of great sincerity, critical reflec-tion, vision and concern.

Introduction

Michael Traber

For ten years and more we have been waiting for the information revolution to occur. All we have got so far are some new pieces of furniture — mainly video cassette recorders at home and micro-computers in the office. They certainly have not 'radically' changed our lives. 'We', of course, are the ordinary men and women forming the 'general public'.

Ralph Lee Smith wrote his book *The Wired Nation* in 1971.[1] Ever since, the popular media as well as academic publications have predicted a 'revolution' which would bring about fundamental changes in economic, political, social and cultural relations — in short, 'the most total revolution that the human race has witnessed since the Industrial Revolution'.[2] In its wake there should have been such benefits as socially relevant information and entertainment for the aged, the handicapped, and linguistic and cultural minorities — thanks to a multiplicity of channels on cable television. Certainly, cable TV has come to some places in some countries, and the wiring of nations continues, although at a much slower pace than antici-pated. But instead of the promised new diet, cable TV simply offers more of the same old programmes.

Cable TV should also have given us better protection. At the push of a button we should have been able to call the police, the fire brigade or a doctor. And what about electronic shopping and banking? Where has that happened? Where is the video phoning and teleconferencing that was to reduce travel and increase face-to-face communication? Where is the cultural differentiation in program-ming, offering us genuine alternatives to programme patterns of the 'lowest common denominator'? Education, too, should have been revolutionized; yet it is still pretty much the same, except for a drop in standards.

The worst disappointment is that governments have still not started to consult their citizens on a great many weighty matters with a yes/no electronic show of hands. Instead, there seems to be less and less participation in political decision-making. We now stay at home to watch our favourite soap opera rather than attend a local government or party political meeting. The 'information explosion' might, at least, have had the effect of keeping citizens better informed: what is actually happening is a rapid growth in misinfor-mation and disinformation. Witness Donna Demac's book, *Keeping*

1

America Uninformed, or Henry Porter's exposure of Fleet Street newspapers, *Lies, Damned Lies.*[3] Clearly, the information revolution has not yet arrived and is nowhere yet in sight, except in the offices of stockbrokers, bankers, spy masters, meteorologists and the headquarters of transnational companies.

There are, of course, many explanations for this. Lack of consumer demand is one. Although more than half the homes in the USA have cable TV, with 60 percent of those having access to between 30 and 53 channels, there is an 'apparently insatiable demand for more entertainment programming' than for diversified and alternative channels.[4] So, at any rate, we are led to believe. Another factor is the lack of capital for the development of the sophisticated two-way structure needed for services like shopping, banking and yes/no opinion polls. Whether such 'risk capital' can ever be found is not clear.

The second great technological development which is said to be going to change our lives is the communication satellite. Some 50 television channels transmitted by satellite are now available to US cable operators and some 20 channels to viewers in Western Europe. But what has changed? There is more sport, more films and more pop music. There has also been a slight increase in news and children's programmes — many of them of questionable value.

Perhaps the real change will come with direct broadcast satellites (DBS). But apparently even DBS has run into difficulties. The problem is cost. It takes US $400 million to build and launch a high-powered communication satellite of the type that can span continental USA. Finance for such satellites seems hard to come by unless antenna dishes are available to receive programmes; and yet it is unlikely that dish antennas will become available before such satellites are launched and are transmitting good programmes.

Another problem for the satellite revolution is standards: this time not programme standards, but equipment. Signals from different satellite operators are not compatible. They could, of course, be made so through inter-government regulations. But this seems unlikely at a time when institutions like British Telecom are being sold off to the private sector, and when 'deregulation' in the USA has become the order of the day. For the time being, the dream of receiving signals directly from a variety of satellites remains just that.

While the information revolution has not yet reached the general public, it is certainly part of the world of the powerful and mighty. 'Clearly, the development of two-way interactive systems in financial offices has been the most dramatic development in the last five years,' Gerald Kline wrote in 1985.[5] Herbert Schiller argues in this volume that 'Today, international affairs are the affairs of the world business system' — thanks to the linking of satellites with computer data bases. The information revolution is also firmly in place for the military establishments, where it in fact began.

All this has far-reaching consequences, but not in the direction of human emancipation and liberation, or of improving the quality of life for ordinary people. If anything, the communication revolution is turning out to be an exercise in consolidating the military, economic and political powers of the elite. In particular, it is of the greatest importance to a hundred or so transnational corporations, most of which have their headquarters in the USA. Rapid collection and transmission of data made the global expansion of the transnational conglomerates possible in the first place. In that sense it has changed global economy, global politics and global military strategy.

The main obstacle to further penetration by the transnational companies has been the reaction of certain stubborn nations in possession of their own post, telephone and telegraph (PTT) systems. But the odds are in favour of the transnationals. First, the big transnational firms own much of what is in the sky. They not only manufacture communication satellites and the hardware of data banks, but also service them and keep them operational, in close cooperation with their military counterparts. If a national PTT organization wishes to make use of a satellite for telecommunications, it will in most cases have to deal with one of these companies.

The second reason giving the transnational corporations the winning edge lies in the weakness of many nation-states. They are either too small and economically weak, or they find it difficult to harness regional economic power. Worst of all, many are ruled or administered by local bourgeoisies who value their own and their countries' adoption by corporate business more than their independence. This problem is keenly felt by the African, Asian and Latin American contributors to this volume, and is the premise for the various courses of action they propose.

Possession of the hardware and control over software, as well as the carving up of institutions (such as PTT systems) which were part and parcel of a nation's sovereignty, have led to an exclusiveness which characterizes much of the information revolution. It has been estimated that about 90 percent of all data flow via satellite systems is intra-corporate, and about 50 percent of all *trans-border* data flow takes place within the communication networks of individual transnational corporations.[6] Add to this the trans-border information flow of the military, and of diplomats, and you have a 'closed sky', an 'information implosion' rather than explosion, all sealed and contained in a corporate world of secrecy.

Satellites, nevertheless, have brought some benefits to the general public, the best of which is a highly efficient international telephone network. But this again needs qualification. Who uses the telephone, and who has the money to pay for international calls? Even with all the money in the world, at this stage it is still barely possible to telephone from London such scholars as Dr Ansah in Ghana, or Dr Reddi in India, both contributors to this book. Nor is there much hope that the telephone will come to rural Africa or India in the foreseeable future. More than 80 percent of the world's international telephone traffic is conducted by the Western industrialized countries,[7] while the vast majority of humankind will remain without domestic facilities for a long time to come, let alone gain access to other satellite-based services.

Too often we forget that

> the new information technologies were developed *in*, *by* and *for* highly advanced capitalist economies — that of the USA in particular. It is to be expected, therefore, that these technologies are now being employed single-mindedly to serve market objectives. Control of the labour force, higher productivity, capture of world markets, and continued capital accumulation are the propelling influences under which the new information technologies are developed.[8]

Which brings us to the main argument of this volume: there is a need for a genuine rather than a phoney revolution, a communication revolution from below. Several contributors, but particularly Mina Ramirez of the Philippines, Moema Viezzer of Brazil and Paul Ansah of Ghana, argue in favour of culturally relevant, development-orientated communication which starts with grassroot organizations. Unless a communication revolution is in the hands and hearts of marginalized groups — such as Filipino cigarette vendors, farmers, fishermen and women's groups, who use their own resources to try to change the status quo — it hardly deserves to be called a 'revolution', but rather a *counter*-revolution.

The communication of such people is now often called 'alternative' — alternative to what people receive from above. Alternative communication, it would seem, is the right way to respond to the communication challenge of our time — not only in the developing countries of the South, but also in the industrialized regions of the North and of South-east Asia. The issue is no longer how to influence or gain access to the information networks of corporate business or powerful governments. In Paul Ansah's words, the goal is the Decolonization of information, Democratization, Demonopolization, and grassroot Development. The communication revolution starts with these four Ds.

But between the high technology of the transnational conglomerates and the 'small media' of the grassroot movements lie the established mass media. They still present a formidable challenge. They are, in part, subsidiaries of the transnational communication empires. In their way of operation, they have become almost a law unto themselves. Willy-nilly, even grassroot groups depend on them for information and, in some cases, entertainment. They are all-pervasive in the industrialized North; but in Africa, most of Asia and much of Latin America, they are still a prerogative of the urbanites. To possess a television set or receive a daily newspaper is still the privilege of a few in most countries of the South. But there is likely to be a slow and consistent spread of the mass media, both electronic and print, into the rural areas. The most striking examples of mass media growth (of considerable significance to mass media researchers) are China and India.[9]

The principal development, however, will be in languages other than English. Will the transnational news and culture industry be able to break the language barriers? China will hardly be a market for their software; and India in future will have only a limited demand for it. But elsewhere, the mass media of the South will, to a large extent, continue to depend on the transnational culture and advertising industries. Therefore, they will continue to finance indirectly part of the high tech enterprises of these corporations.

In the end, governments in many developing countries have considerable leverage over the future of communication. So have the national PTT systems in Europe. Developing communication policies for the future is one of their most urgent tasks. In most cases such policies will be ineffective on the national level alone, as they can be formulated and implemented only on the regional level, particularly in Africa and Latin America. Apart from developing grassroots communication, new national and regional information policies are a high priority for all those who want to see life after the 'information revolution'.

Many of the thoughts and strategies reflected in this book have been part of the daily life and discussion of a London office where eighteen people from twelve different nations work on communication projects and communication issues. The hub in the wheel of the World Association for Christian Communication (WACC) has been Dr Hans W. Florin, its General Secretary since 1976. Under his leadership we have moved a long way in our thinking and planning, in our concerns for people and their cultures, in our hopes for genuine development, human rights, justice and peace. Now that he is leaving the WACC, this book is dedicated to Dr Florin as a token of gratitude and appreciation from his co-workers, and from some 600 members of a worldwide association committed to the communication revolution from below.

6 *The myth of the information revolution*

Notes

1. Ralph Lee Smith, *The Wired Nation*. New York: Longman, 1972.
2. Teresita Z. Hermano (ed.), *Communication Challenges of Our Times: An Asian Perspective*. Manila: World Association for Christian Communication, 1985.
3. Donna A. Demac, *Keeping America Uninformed: Government Secrecy in the 1980s*. New York: Pilgrim Press, 1984; Henry Porter, *Lies, Damned Lies, Fleet St. Exposed*. London: Chatto, 1984.
4. F. Gerald Kline, 'The Wired Nation and the Eye in the Sky — Where are These New Technologies of Entertainment and Information Going?' in *Rundfunk and Fernsehen*, 1985, 33(3–4):409.
5. *ibid.*, p. 412.
6. Meheroo Jussawalla, 'Constraints on Economic Analysis of Transborder Data Flows', in *Media, Culture and Society*, 1985, 7(3):299–300.
7. Edward W. Ploman, *Space, Earth and Communication*. London: Frances Pinter, 1984.
8. Herbert I. Schiller, 'Strengths and Weaknesses of the New International Information Empire', in Philip Lee (ed.), *Communication For All*. New York: Orbis, 1985.
9. See *Media Development* (London), 33(1), February 1986, which is devoted to the theme of 'Communication in China', and Paul Hartmann, B.R. Patil and B.C. Agrawal (eds), *The Role of Mass Communication in Indian Village Life*. New Delhi: Sage, 1986.

1

Is there life after the information revolution?

Cees J. Hamelink

A myth is a story through which the world is explained to us. When confronted with a myth, we should scrutinize its contents on two levels: realism and ideology. A responsible attitude towards a myth demands critical questioning of whether its contents stand up to reality, and of whose interests it legitimizes. This is important, because stories about the world never originate in a void: they always represent a pre-selected point of view embedded in an existential position. In this way, the myth transcends its descriptive brief and acquires a normative dimension. The myth also tells us how the world ought to be, and provides us with moral categories that indicate what kind of behaviour is desirable and what kind of acts are objectionable.

The myth of the information society

In contemporary society — almost worldwide — a powerful myth is being persuasively told by numerous story-tellers. It is the myth of the information society. This myth offers an explanation of the world of the late twentieth century and presents the normative implications of its historical interpretation. It suggests that the 'information revolution' is the most significant historical development of our time: a revolutionary transition to a fundamentally different age.

This transition is the shift from an industrial society to an information society. Related descriptions of this new society include 'post-industrial', 'post-capitalist', 'post-ideological' and 'post-protestant'. Whatever term is used, the main feature of the transition is the increased relevance of the resource called 'information'. In the information society, this resource is basic to all processes. For example, the processing of information is seen to be a major contributing factor to the economic development of societies.

The most important aspect of the myth is the notion that we are entering a radically different stage of human history. The information society is a 'post-society': it means a break with previous values, social arrangements and modes of production. The tone of the myth is 'computopian': it expects that the application of computer-steered technologies will effectively terminate a social structure which is characterized by an endless struggle between winners and losers, between rulers and ruled.

The myth of the information society has three dimensions: economic, political and cultural.

Economy. The information society will witness the end of the capitalist, industrial production with its inherent vices of centralization, expansion, standardization, synchronization, and exploitation. There will be a shift from industrial production to the provision of services in a de-monopolized and diversified market.

Politics. The political arena of the information society is participatory. Its decision-making is decentralized and its insistence on greater access to information for all its citizens equates with the shift of power from the governing elite to the real democratic process of the push-button referendum.

Culture. In the information society, the misery of labour is taken away from the human being and appropriated by the electronic system; flexible and smart robots create unprecedented leisure time. In this Garden of Eden, people enjoy the autonomous production of a diversity of cultural products. The massive culture of the industrial society gives way to the individualist cultural consumption of products at times and in places that people choose themselves.

The realism of the myth

Does the myth provide us with an explanation of our times that survives critical historical X-raying? The realistic quality of the myth depends largely on the plausibility of the historical watershed it assumes. However, history may, on serious reflection, and despite all the revolutionary notions of its interpreters, turn out to be more of a continuous process than 'new age' prophets are willing to accept. What we experience in our time could be explained as a mere continuation of a historical process that does not have one fixed and uncontested point of departure. Rather than thinking in terms of revolutionary change from the past, the information society could be described as a logical successor to previous historical phases. What is termed 'information revolution' could, in a more sober analysis, be seen as equally *non*-revolutionary as its predecessor, the industrial revolution.

Some two hundred years ago, in some parts of the world, mechanical techniques began to be used increasingly in the production and distribution of industrial goods. This mechanization process — largely motivated by considerations of cost efficiency — logically evolved in several stages of upgrading, such as rationalization (Taylorism) and conveyor belt automation (Fordism). Technical developments, for example in the field of energy utilization, assist this process of refinement. Mechanical techniques, however, require capital-intensive energy in the form of manual labour or fossil fuel. The logic of cost efficiency supports their replacement by semi-independent systems that have minimal energy requirements and yield better cost-benefit ratios. Thus, electronic systems utilizing information rather than energy input come to substitute for machines. This process can be called informatization: mechanical techniques are increasingly replaced by information techniques in the production and distribution of industrial goods.

On the surface, this suggests the transition to a totally new type of economy: the service economy. Informatization implies the disappearance of industry, and it is certainly true that in many developed countries (as well as in some of the industrializing ones) the service sector contributes considerably to the national economy.

In the developing countries, the contribution to the GNP by services has increased from an average 41 percent in 1960 to an average 44.2 percent in 1981. In the same period, however, industrial contribution to GNP also grew, from 32.4 to 36.8 percent. In the industrial market economies, by contrast, the industrial contribution declined from 40 to 36 percent and services increased from 54 to 61 percent. Many services, though, are integrally related to industrial production and distribution and could not survive in a de-industrialized economy. Therefore, on balance, there is no real indication that the significance of industrial production is withering away. (Figures are from World Bank Development Reports.)

At this point it should also be recalled that the technical innovations that contribute to so-called revolutionary change (such as computers, robots, satellites) are 'new' only if the world is seen a-historically. Technical developments in real history cannot be described as 'breakthroughs' — they always have long histories of conceptual and practical preparation.

The question arises whether the historical process in which informatization evolves from mechanization implies fundamental changes in the social structures in which it takes place. To answer this it is helpful to go back to that earlier phase in history which is commonly referred to as the industrial revolution. The application of mechanical techniques to industrial production is usually associated with an important social transformation: the shift of power from the feudal lord to the capitalist entrepreneur. On the surface, this was accompanied by important social changes in the technical instruments which people used (the change from tools to machines), in the social landscape (the emergence of factories and means of transportation) and in the life-styles of many people (the creation of an industrial proletariat).

What did not change were the power relationships between winners and losers, between rulers and ruled. These only acquired new names. The serf became the worker. The serf lived in poverty, disease and misery: so did the worker. If anything, the worker was worse off, because the contractual arrangements between serf and lord offered more security than the worker–entrepreneur equivalent.

Different techniques were used, but access to their management was not radically altered. What is striking is that there is no indication that the situation will be any different with the arrival of the information society. Changes can certainly be expected, but they will be limited to the instruments that societies deploy (computers, robots), the social landscape (the paperless office and the humanless factory) and people's life-styles (changes in notions of privacy, the risk of unemployment, the need to become computer-literate). This is certainly extremely important for the individual citizens affected, but it is by no means a social revolution.

It is usually argued that, in the transition from an agricultural society to an industrial society, and from an industrial society to an information society, the sources of social power shift. It may be that the sources of power changed from land ownership to capital ownership, and from capital ownership to information ownership; but what fundamental difference does this make when, after every shift, there is a new elite (usually evolving from the old one) controlling access to the source of power?

The myth of the information society claims that, whereas access to land and capital was restricted, *everyone* can own information. A number of factors militate against this simplistic statement.

1. In certain social sectors information is becoming increasingly complex and specialist. In general this implies that, despite an increased volume of available information, more people know less.

2. The resource 'information' is far more difficult to exploit than land or capital. It demands highly developed intellectual and managerial skills which are very unevenly distributed in society.

3. Advanced hardware and software for information-processing are expensive and can be afforded only by land owners or capital owners. The rest will have to try to catch up using obsolete instruments.

4. Information becomes a source of power only if the necessary infrastructure for its production, processing, storing, retrieval and transportation is accessible.

5. The myth assumes that people were never able to exert power because they were ill-informed. However, too often people knew precisely what was wrong and unjust, and were very well informed

about the misconduct of their rulers. Yet they did not act, and their information did not become a source of power, because they lacked the material and strategic means for revolt.

6. Control over and access to advances in information technology are very unevenly distributed in the world, and the fact that millions of individuals can fiddle with their home computers does not change this. The management structure of the information industry is not affected by the proliferation of electronic gadgets. If anything, it is considerably strengthened by the widespread use of its products.

Today, as with the subsequent interpretation of the impact of the industrial revolution, we are once again confronted with the false claim of a historical watershed. Such 'transitions', 'shifts' or 'revolutions' are often more representative of academic arguments than historical reality. We do not have medievalists because there were the Middle Ages; rather, we have a period described as the Middle Ages because we have medievalists. Moreover, historical transitions usually describe the power shifts from one governing elite to another. History is commonly recorded and interpreted as the history of elites. It is the history of kings and popes and their palaces and cathedrals, of admirals and generals and their endeavours. History tells us very little about those who were governed by the elites: the ruled, the losers, the exploited, the millions. A historical record written from their perspective would reveal that for them the historical, revolutionary transitions meant no basic alteration to their lot. Their way of relating to the social structure was not revolutionized but remained the same, and occasionally even deteriorated in such a remarkable 'upthrust into barbarism' (Lewis Mumford) as characterized the nineteenth century.

If we apply these insights to the introduction of information technology, they may serve to qualify revolutionary expectations. The invention and application of the printing press is usually perceived as revolutionary. It shifted power from the privileged possessors of information, and it made information a widely accessible resource. In reality, however, for several centuries after Gutenberg, millions remained illiterate, and even when they learned to read, it did not mean that they had access to the art of writing. Even where illiteracy has disappeared today (though it is unlikely that any country in the twentieth century — despite the statistics — has achieved universal literacy), millions are still only semi-literate. The printing press never became the instrument of the losers; rather, it developed as the essential weapon in the struggle between aristocracy and bourgeoisie. The shift from oral culture to print culture did not serve the interests of the 'grassroots' of European history. Traditional oral cultures had a participatory character — the fairy tales and folk stories were told by the narrator, but the audience contributed suggestions, embellishments and additions. The print culture is largely passive. An educated elite speaks to an audience that is no longer communal but individualized. The printed fairy tale of the eighteenth century is the moralistic contribution of aristocrats telling the bourgeoisie how to behave.

In summary, we need to ask who has benefited from what the historical records label 'revolution'? For whom did it alter, let alone improve, life? There may be waves of civilization (as Alvin Toffler suggests), but that is small solace to those who continue to drown!

The ideological quality of the myth

The myth of the information society has a crucial normative implication in that it equates technical progress with a qualitative improvement to human life. This leap from quantitative growth to qualitative growth is used to sanction unrestrained technical development for the purpose of material expansion. It obscures the fact that, in the history of technical progress, quantitative increase (the emphasis on 'more') may reduce the quality of life in all its diversity. It also shifts attention from such qualitative questions as 'Why do human beings act like robots?' to such quantitative questions as 'How can we make robots act like humans?' The assumption that material growth and human growth are interrelated also hides the destruction and extermination which has accompanied technical progress, of which Auschwitz and Hiroshima are the dramatic landmarks.

Related to the equation is the normative message of adaptation. Since technical progress is for the betterment and benefit of humankind, society cannot voluntarily choose one way or another. There is only one option: adopt and adapt. This obscures the 'low-grade schizophrenia' (Erich Fromm) of the one-sided, quantitatively oriented, technological society. It renders the pathological phenomenon normal as long as the millions share it. It also steers technical development away from public accountability and critical philosophical enquiry.

Is it likely that these normative messages and their implied obscurantisms serve the interests of the 'losers'? To explore this, we return to the three dimensions of the myth.

Economy. The information techniques deployed in today's societies (and their planned innovations) are the perfect instruments to perpetuate a capitalist mode of production. They offer the support necessary to a cost-effective division of labour, a fragmentation of the production process, integrated control of all facets of production, and optimum use of the management structure of centralized decentralization of the large industrial corporation.

Politics. The development of information technology makes centralized control over decentralized activities simpler than ever before, thus allowing more latitude for deviant political behaviour. Moreover, the link between information technology and democratization is guided by unwarranted expectations about what machines per se can do. This is based on the assumption that giving human beings more machines makes them qualitatively different. This point of view bypasses the significance of the social infrastructure in which humans and machines interact. It is like suggesting that penguins become more human if they are given refrigerators.

Culture. Technical innovations in information tend to support a global process of cultural synchronization rather than autonomous diversity. Illustrations of this are the ubiquitous TV/home video set with its standardized software and the universal logarithm of computer language. Information techniques facilitate the emergence of an oligopolized leisure market that defines and produces cultural services. This leads to a rapid loss of self-defined mechanisms through which people cope with their environment: the core of cultural development.

A sobering footnote to the expected decentralization of economic, political and cultural activities may be found in the fact that they all depend on electricity, that centrally controlled source of vital energy without which information technology cannot function.

All this suggests that the myth of the information society, interpreted historically, is meant to cater to the interests of those who initiate and manage the 'information revolution': the most powerful sectors of society, its central administrative elites, the military establishment and global industrial corporations. But the myth does not hold promises for those who in today's society are the losers. In the information society they will simply be computer-controlled losers.

A counter-myth to act as a balance
Critical analysis of the prevalent myth requires examination of its counterpart. The foregoing can indeed be read as an alternative explanation of historical developments. It can be legitimately asked, therefore, what the normative implication of the counter-myth is.

The counter-myth defends the interests of the losers, thus violating the dominant historical norm. Therefore, it is heretical. In the strict etymological sense this means 'taking sides'. This choice of direction implies a different set of normative imperatives or heretical ethics.

Realism is its point of departure. Critical reflection on its claim to an equally valid place alongside historical, revolutionary transitions is based on that realism.

The counter-myth does not support fundamental transitions, but rather proposes a continuous historical process of changes on the surface and power shifts among the governing elites. These 'changes' do not amount to basic transformations for the historical losers. Information techniques, according to the counter-myth, are a refinement of mechanical technology which are perfectly suited to reinforce a capitalist industrial society.

The counter-myth does not employ the notion of an 'information society'. It considers this device deceptive because it incorrectly suggests the emergence of a society which is radically different from its predecessor. Moreover, it believes that the notion is confusing because it assumes that an increase of signal traffic equals an expansion in the volume of information. What is actually happening, and at an exponential rate, is an increase in the flow of signals which connect more and more nodes in an expanding global grid. Some of these signals will certainly form configurations which have information value. However, we cannot predict which signals will comprise information. This makes the notion of an 'information society' at least premature. If we insist on inventing names for stages in human history, it would be more appropriate in this particular case to refer to that vital resource on which all information processing depends and call it the 'electricity society'.

A basic premise of the counter-myth is that the hierarchical order is integral to the human system. One obvious physiological example of this is the hierarchy of the living organism. Cells, muscles, nerves, organs — all have their intrinsic rhythms and patterns of activity. But they are subordinated as parts to the higher centres in the hierarchy. Regardless of whether we consider galactic systems, living organisms or social organizations, all complex structures and processes of a relatively stable character display hierarchic organization.

Throughout history there have been numerous attempts (heretical movements) to restructure hierarchies: they either died natural deaths, died through co-optation, or only succeeded in swaying the pyramid slightly. Even when the pyramid seemed to be turned upside-down — the case of real revolution — more often than not only the names changed. Power shifts from one social class to another, but the hierarchy remains.

The industrial revolution, like the Russian revolution, did not fundamentally transform the hierarchical order: they were both semantic revolutions. Hierarchy breeds the desire to win. In a hierarchical order only the organisms which are not self-conscious, brainwashed or coerced into slavery do not strive upwards to the more important places in the order. If, as is often the case, this upwards mobility is not successful, the hierarchical escape is downwards to oppression: others are made lower in rank, like the black, the woman, the child.

Human beings are forever competing, either with one another or themselves. Even in relatively cooperative societies there are always hierarchical differences, internally or externally. At the most egalitarian moments of the Chinese revolution there were rulers and ruled, and always the perception that the Chinese were, in the external hierarchy, far superior to the barbarians from the West.

This compulsive competitiveness constrains the human potential for spiritual and moral growth. Its exclusive emphasis on 'more, bigger and better' gives preferential treatment to all those human achievements that can be quantified. It may even constrain human life as such.

Competition aims at the extinction or subjugation of the contender. Its logical conclusion is the absurdity of leaving no one to compete with: the dictator without people to dictate to. But even short of this absurdity, competition leads to irrational behaviour, such as crowds competing to get out of a building on fire, or a person persistently competing with him/herself and ending up a neurotic wreck.

Human beings have been competitive throughout history, but necessarily on a limited scale. That never mattered so much as it does today. The scale of competition used to be limited because:

1. there was only a limited notion of how many potential contributors there were;
2. physical/technical constraints limited the number of competitors that could be eliminated;
3. the environment was perceived as a finite system because the human being was the final point in evolution and the globe was considered a closed system.

Today the scale of competition has dramatically increased because:

1. there are more people (population growth);
2. they all want more (ecologically speaking, there are more competitors for the same resources);
3. the competitors all know about each other (instantaneous and global communications);
4. most physical restraints have been removed in technological development: we can now kill the contender many times over;

LIBRARY ST. MARY'S COLLEGE

5. the environment is now seen as an infinite system: competition has no limits and can now also be extended into space.

As a result, we are confronted with the unprecedented pervasiveness of competition — in such diverse fields as education, physical beauty, and sexual performance. Also, our better intentioned endeavours use the hierarchical metaphor: war on poverty, combat of racism, the fight against illiteracy. And, deceptively as well as perversely, the jargon of the economist suggests the ideal of 'perfect competition'.

Since we are no longer physically restrained in our competitive efforts, we need to rely on moral restraint lest we carry our natural instincts to absurd degrees. This is not a very encouraging conclusion. There is little sign that the world's political leadership is gifted with a high degree of moral maturity. The technological–industrial–military complex asks merely what it can do, not what it should do: its main interest is engineerability, not morality.

It may be true that throughout history human beings have not displayed an impressive record of moral restraint. We may never have seriously restrained ourselves; but once again, it may never have mattered so much as now — at least, not on a world scale. Today it matters globally, and at a time when we seem to have lost much of our capacity for moral restraint.

Two factors are important here. In the course of recent history (approximately the last four centuries) we have increasingly divorced arts and technology, that is, the synthetic and analytical approaches to our environment. The dominant mode of analytical thought — ruthlessly dissecting the environment into smaller and more controllable parts — escaped from the need to fit its exploits into the search for meaning. The analytical mind without the restraints of the synthetic mind thinks that anything goes! The borderline is drawn only by what is materially not feasible.

Related to this is the issue of secularization. In the wake of the separation of state and religion, God was declared dead and all non-empirically verifiable sources of moral concern were abolished. It was a courageous step to tear up the metaphysical maps and take destiny into our own hands. However, if the only orientation which can now be offered is 'more of the same', the whole exercise becomes utterly futile.

Heretical ethics
The normative implications of the counter-myth are heretical in the sense that they propose transcending the hierarchical order of the world thrusting itself into infinite competition. They also raise the

issue of moral restraint when the world thought it had liberated itself from moral demands and was able to conduct its own business. The most the counter-myth asks is that we overcome the constraint of our natural make-up; the least it asks is that we deliberately restrain our compulsive competitive neurosis. Since nothing less than human survival is at stake, it befits a complex age such as ours that there are various options to resolve our predicament. A rapidly expanding body of literature presents a wealth of Utopian vistas, of which a brief investigation reveals the following models.

1. *Interventionism*. Under this heading one finds those materialists or spiritualists who propose to 'make' tomorrow's world through some form of external engineering. The material engineers depart from the mundane assumption of the 'technological fix': they are forever curing symptoms without ever getting close to the organism's basic constraints. The spiritual engineers, who tirelessly build the networks for the 'new age', employ admittedly less trivial and more organic premises and consciously substitute the notion of curing the symptoms with that of healing the system. Yet their insistence on 'holism' (despite its importance for joining the analytic and synthetic modes of thought) may contribute to the failure to recognize the essence of our plight. They project an original universal harmony (unity, one-ness of the ontological structure) that in the course of history fell prey to such Greek and Cartesian dichotomies as body and soul, mind and matter. The reunion of what history has separated leads to the harmony of the final perspective, expressed in the togetherness of lambs and wolves, or similar symbolic images. This route does not help the transformation of the hierarchical order. It may easily solve the problem by ignoring it and may usher the world into another semantic revolution. Holistic visions bypass the fact that the ontological structure is hierarchical: not united but divided. Much more is at stake here than philosophical niceties. It discloses the unsettling uncertainty of an irresolvable problem.

2. *Self-regulation*. Under this heading one finds those who believe that God, the market or the MAD doctrine will restrain the system from totally destroying itself. This approach is not helpful either. However sophisticated the mechanism of self-adaptation, it is basically limited by the organism it controls. A thermostat can regulate a system but cannot fundamentally alter it.

How, then, do we go about challenging the natural order? Primarily by not externalizing the origin of the hierarchical mode. We tend to recognize the outsider as the source of competition: the state, the communists, the capitalists, the neighbours, the instructors, the parents. When people claim that the world would have been different if all these external factors had been different, they should also consider that in that case they would not have been there either. We need to recognize the hierarchical order in our 20,000 genes, and to explore whether sustained non-hierarchical behaviour might not, in the long run, alter our genetic make-up. Without resorting to crude behaviourism, it would seem possible that we could breed non-hierarchical impulses and responses in our organisms. Hardly anywhere have we made a serious start to this. Even where we train people to behave cooperatively, it usually serves the purpose of external competition. 'The best team wins!'

We are very skilled at forms of deceit in which competition is made to look like cooperation. One illustration is the anomaly of the handshake after a tennis match. This is a totally misplaced and misleading gesture. The only real promising humane gesture would be to play cooperative tennis, which our moral immaturity fails to perceive as sufficiently exciting. If we want to survive, we have to remove competitive pressures from our daily endeavours and start experiencing the joy and excitement of non-competitive behaviour.

In addition to this survival strategy, we need to rid ourselves of the compulsion to take advantage. Whenever we sense an opportunity, we seize it. We feel that what we *can* do, we *should* do. It would show great moral growth if we learned to choose not to do automatically what we are capable of doing. In this regard the ecological movement has already shown promising examples. We should also improve our moral capacity by finding a complementarity between the analytic and the synthetic mind, between arts and technology. Here the feminist movement has already taken the lead.

We must understand that heretical ethics of this kind face powerful resistance which may well crush any initiative to restructure the hierarchical order. First, there are vested interests in the existing order from resourceful social actors, such as industrial and financial conglomerates. It is naive to believe that they can be transformed as if we were merely dealing with the minor aberrations of otherwise fine institutions. They are the very representatives of the dangerously competitive order that should be discarded.

Despite their power, these institutions are not monolithic entities and are fraught with contradictions. They find it increasingly difficult to make people believe that they deliver what they promise in the face of the failures of the pharmaceutical, nutrition, defence and information industries to heal, feed, protect and inform the world. Their competitive drive leads to ever larger combines in which competitors are 'eaten up', leaving no one to compete with. Their vast scale of operations and the implied need for reliable electronic networks make them vulnerable to information leaks, system apraxia and external sabotage. The social forces representing the hierarchical order can be seen as dinosaurs. Enormously powerful yet unable to survive, their own size and strength will be the cause of their downfall.

Therefore, heretical ethics approaches these forces with neither collaboration, internal transformation nor head-on collision in mind, but employing a 'judo strategy': exploiting, in a calculated manner, the strength and weight of the opponent.

Second, there is a complex counterforce in human psychology. What M. Maccoby has called the 'death-wish syndrome' refers to those who need the excitement of competition because its ultimate risk is death. If one takes the illustration of competitive behaviour in traffic, it seems highly plausible that many people are indeed willing to gamble their lives away. There is also moral immaturity in many countries where dying for 'king and country' is seen as an act of courage. Yet however true this may be, there is comfort in the idea that perhaps only very few of us are ready to play Russian roulette.

Another explanation of this unwillingness to give up competitiveness may be found in the increasing artificiality of our lives. We are creating a thoroughly artificial environment which requires little conscious living. The artefacts of our time facilitate an ordered and secure existence (electronic household appliances, electronic music instruments, digital alarm clocks and around-the-clock electronic surveillance). This demands more and more excessive emotions in response to make people feel that they are still alive. On this basis, one may expect that the more artefacts a society employs, the more pervasive its need for 'death-wish' behaviour will be.

Here again, heretical ethics would warn that we have developed and deployed artefacts without restraint. Whatever we could do, we did; and what was available, we acquired. Heretical ethics would ask people to reflect on the productive or destructive implications of such artefacts as the digital watch. Why should we not say 'no' to the superfluous and deceptive precision of the time-keeping it imposes on us?

Today's technological capacity enables us to follow our natural order to absurd limits. Yet, despite this possibility, we have not really harnessed our capacity for moral restraint. We are, in fact, actors in the drama of Dr Frankenstein, which exposes the moral inadequacy of the scientist to deal with what he creates. Our age allows Frankenstein to do exactly what he likes in his laboratory. It permits the limitless expansion of the analytical mind, conceals the competitive neurosis, and stifles spiritual growth.

We have taken fate in our hands, but we have no real sense of direction. We have liberated ourselves from worldly and otherworldly toil, but we do not know what to do with our newly acquired freedom. Even worse, we have lost the capacity to reflect on what we should be doing with it. We need, therefore, to stop celebrating utopian scenarios, and stop worrying unduly about the monsters we may be creating. It is time, instead, that we tried to heal Dr Frankenstein!

Life after the 'information revolution' will depend on the success or failure of our therapy.

2

The erosion of national sovereignty by the world business system

Herbert I. Schiller

Today, international affairs are the affairs of the world business system. Powerful business enclaves within the nation-state have moved outside it as well. The last half of the twentieth century, especially since World War II, has seen the phenomenal growth of the transnational corporation, a business with operations carried on in several different global sites. The *Business Roundtable*, a publication that speaks for the most powerful US companies, including those that are most active outside the continental boundaries, emphasizes this development:

> In the 1960s, the US corporations responded to a growing world market by expanding at an astounding rate. During the period 1960–1976, the average multinational enterprise established or acquired four new foreign manufacturing subsidiaries in more than ten countries.[1]

At the present time, the transnational company is the dominant economic unit in the world economy. A few thousand companies account for an ever-increasing share of the international output of goods and services.

This economic infrastructure of the world economy is not yet complete. The more powerful and energetic transnational companies are striving to capture entire slices of the international market, sectors that encompass more than individual products and services. In this latest growth stage, some transnational corporations aim to consolidate whole chunks of social and economic activity under their domain.

This is most observable in consumption goods, entertainment activities, financial services and, most recently, industrial manufacturing. For example, in international travel, numerous related activities are being integrated into global corporate enterprises, which 'process' the traveller from departure to destination. United Airlines (UAL) is a case in point. With its latest acquisitions — Pan American Airways and Hertz Car Rental Company — UAL, already the largest domestic airline in the USA, transformed itself into a worldwide company owning also a luxury hotel chain, Westin. Altogether, UAL is now in a position to provide the traveller with a complete service from departure to arrival almost anywhere in the world.

Possibly more basic still are developments in the industrial sphere. The recent purchase by General Motors (GM), the second largest industrial corporation in the USA, of Hughes Aircraft, after having earlier acquired Electronic Data Systems, puts GM into a commanding position to design and introduce electronic systems not only into the production of motor cars but into the entire industrial system, on a global as well as a domestic basis.

Finally, though by no means exhaustively, consider the expectations of IBM, the dominating force in the computer business, both in the USA and abroad. John F. Akers, the new chief executive, made some predictions at the beginning of 1985, on his assumption of office, that in no way can be considered fanciful. 'The industry', he said, 'will be in ten years probably the biggest industry in the world.' And he calculated that IBM's revenues would increase from 1984's $46 billion to an estimated $180 billion-plus a decade later.[2]

The dollar value of economic activity that this last figure represents exceeds that of the entire individual national output of the great majority of nations. Actually, all but a handful of advanced, industrial countries come nowhere near this level of activity.

The gargantuan size of these global private enterprises, and the extension of their functions, are the striking features of capitalism in the waning years of the twentieth century. Equally remarkable, all of this would be out of the question without the developments in communication and information technologies over the last half-century. Without the new instrumentation — communication satellites, computer and computer networks, fibre optics and television — the present scope of worldwide business (and military) activity, organized by centrally controlled economic and political empires, would be impossible.

The maintenance of these global systems is totally dependent on the instantaneous, heavy-volume, transmission of data and information flows. Again, the *Business Roundtable* makes explicit the importance of information technology to its powerful constituency:

> The dependence of multinational corporations — whether they are pursuing intracorporate functions or providing services or both — upon international information transfer is increasing. A 1983 survey, with 380 companies from 85 countries participating, indicates that 94 per cent of the corporations now use, or are planning to use, international computer-to-computer communications systems.[3]

The information technology that is at the disposal of the transnational company enables it to be in immediate and continual contact with its plants and branches around the world for '(i) financial reporting and consolidation; (ii) financial management; (iii) marketing; (iv) distribution; (v) order processing; (vi) research and development; (vii) various clerical functions'.[4]

Altogether, the conclusion is beyond dispute. '[T]elecommunications is central to the operation of all multinational business activity.'[5] This too is the conclusion of Walter Wriston, former chairman of Citibank, the world's largest banking corporation. Wriston writes, 'an awareness is beginning to grow about the extent to which our world relies on the free flow of data across national boundaries.'[6] From this ensues one of the major consequences of the melding of transnational business and information.

National sovereignty

The massive utilization of information technology on behalf of the transnationalization of economic activity has effects that transcend economic impacts, though these are fundamental in their own right. Parallel with the progress of transnationalization is the progressive erosion of national sovereignty. What is meant by national sovereignty is the capability of a nation-state's leaders to make policies that arise from, and represent, internal (domestic) interests, whether these interests be oligarchic, democratic, egalitarian or some combination thereof.

The undermining of national sovereignty generally appears to be an inescapable and even non-purposive outcome of transnationalization. Actually, the managers of the transnational order are quite deliberate in their efforts to undercut national determination and decision-making. Rarely do they overlook an opportunity to disparage the concept itself, to say nothing of engaging in activities that greatly weaken it. Walter Wriston, for example, approvingly writes: 'The ancient and basic concept of sovereignty which has been discussed since the time of Plato is being profoundly changed by information technology.'[7]

Voicing the corporate view as well, the *Business Roundtable* is unequivocal about where its priorities are. 'The sovereign rights of nations to determine their own telecommunication policies is not the issue; rather, it is the international consequences of these national policies that may be subject to legitimate challenge by other countries whose interests are adversely affected.'[8]

What the *Roundtable* people are asserting here is that a problem occurs when nation-states establish national policies for their own protection. It is these that must be challenged, not those actions that attack national oversight. It is also notable that in this formulation the *Roundtable* expresses a transnational corporate view but packages it in a wrapper of its own nation-state's interests.

Undermining the economic sector of national sovereignty

Why is national sovereignty anathema to transnational business? At bottom, it is explained by the longstanding insistence of capital to do what it will, with no accountability whatsoever. This has been a cardinal principle of capitalism from the beginning. Wherever capital exists as an organized system of production, it strives for what it likes to call 'freedom'. In practice, this means its ability to pursue its own interests — accumulation from profit-taking — without hindrance.

The historical record demonstrates that since the beginnings of capitalism, at least half a millenium ago, there have been efforts, increasing over time, to reduce and limit capital's range of free action. The struggle proceeds, differently from locale to locale. In the twentieth century, in the advanced industrial capitalist countries, interventions in economic resource allocation — a serious infringement on capitalism's 'freedom' — have been frequent and continuing. They have been most evident immediately after the profound world economic crisis in the late 1920s and 1930s.

In the present era, transnational capital differs in no way from earlier stages in its insistence on as much unhindered activity as possible. What *is* different is its capability to manoeuvre more adroitly in pursuit of its objective: unchecked capital accumulation.

It bears repeating that this capability resides in its unprecedentedly great mobility, provided largely by modern information and communication technologies. Its decision-making on a global scale, made possible by instantaneous information flows and data transfers, is at the same time the source of the deepening crisis of the nation-state and its loss of authority, everywhere in the world.

The master mechanism of any economic system is found in its means of resource allocation — where, and if, investments will be made; where production will be undertaken or abandoned; what share of the product will go to labour; who will bear the tax burden; and similar basic decisions.

It is in the allocation of resources that the power of capital is exerted. When capital has its way, resource allocation decisions are made for its benefit, and it prospers at the expense of the rest of the population, especially the working population.

As we have mentioned, in most countries of advanced capitalism, during the twentieth century a number of restraints have been imposed on capital, to protect the stability of the overall system in general and the more vulnerable elements of the population — the young, the old, the sick and the disabled — in particular. These measures were effected by the state, reacting to the pressure of the disadvantaged groups whose lives had been made intolerable in the crisis period.

In this last quarter of the twentieth century, the era of transnational capital, these measures of modest general protection and equity, as well as the state's authority to enforce them, are at risk. Capital, at both the national and international level, has gained enormous strength, and the flexibility and mobility to exercise it.

The international information flows, also called transborder data flows (TDF), that the new information technology permits, enable a transnational enterprise to make resource allocation decisions which are able to elude national jurisdictions. This may happen to even the most powerful state apparatuses. Recent trends in the USA are indicative. For a variety of reasons, one of which is the overpriced US dollar, American companies have been transferring production overseas. The *Wall Street Journal* reports that 'the list of US companies shifting production abroad is a long and growing one. . . . Ford Motor Co., Du Pont Co., Ingersoll-Rand, Goodyear Tire and Rubber Co. . . .'[9]

In this instance, the cause seems to be the strong US dollar — which makes foreign sites cheaper to operate and to compete from. In other cases, it is the price of labour and, equally important, the strength of the labour movement to demand a larger share of the product.

But, for the moment at least, labour's strength has been checkmated by transnational capital. With the existing means of communication, capital can, with relative ease, shift production from one site to another and play off one (national) group of workers against another. The outcome of these tricks is job insecurity, lower wages all around, and increased transnational corporate profits and authority.

How this is accomplished is the subject of the following account:

> A union is concerned with workers in its country: a multinational corporation knows no bounds. While the chief executive can look to the far corners of his realm through the screen of a desk-top terminal, the unionist still hesitates to make an international phone call. While a shop steward dickers with a plant manager, the plant's destiny may be determined on another continent.

The reporter adds that a European Community proposal that would compel multinationals 'to tell workers in advance about plans that would change their lives and ask their opinions' has little chance of adoption. US business especially opposes it, because, 'worst of all', it 'could lead to the establishment of transnational bargaining'.[10]

From the perspective of transnational capital, this is precisely what has to be avoided. 'The guiding principle at Xerox,' the same account states, 'is that industrial relations with workers in any one country are kept strictly separate from relations with workers in any other country'.[11]

It is the capability to shift production, capital, data, whatever, without accounting to anyone at all, that presently affords capital its great advantage over labour, national and international. At the same time, it is this same capability that renders national efforts to provide protection of home industry, jobs and the general stability of the domestic economy increasingly futile.

Still other techniques contribute to the same end. The evolution of the world market, dominated by transnational corporate enterprise, has led to new ways to organize production efficiently. An account of current manufacturing and industrial organizational methods in the transnationalized economy is instructive:

> Another strategy used by manufacturing firms to compete effectively in the world market is 'focused production'. Instead of each plant producing a whole line of products, one plant produces one product, or even one basic component, while other plants assemble components into specialized products. *This means of manufacturing also depends upon the unhampered flow of information among the company's various branches. Similarly, the ability to coproduce in other countries depends upon access to common data bases, which are usually located in the US, because a product cannot be manufactured from two different sets of specifications.*[12]

In what seems to be strictly a decision based on productive efficiency — to concentrate one product or component line in one or several factories, in different countries, owned by the same transnational company — a number of astonishing control elements are achieved.

The country in which the one product/component factory is located can hardly feel confident that it has been given comprehensive mastery of the production process. If anything, it is merely a site for the operation of a partial process of production, which might be shifted or halted at any time, at the direction of the external decision-maker. Even if the host country decided to take over the plant, what would be its value? It represents only part of a complex production process.

More remarkable still, the know-how, the specifications of the (limited) production function, residing in the electronic data base are located *outside* the host country, available to local managers only at the discretion of central headquarters. By the same token, the instructions (specifications) can be interrupted and cut off, at any time, by orders from afar. In fact, one blatant example of an arbitrary termination of data base access — to the local subsidiary of a US transnational company — occurred in the Dresser Industries (France) case. In that instance, the US government ordered the cut-off to penalize France for continuing to fulfil its contract in supplying equipment for the Euro-Siberian pipeline with the Soviet Union.[13]

'Focused production' and centralized data base control, however efficient they may be, are antithetical to national sovereignty.

Financial and information flows

Still another economic phenomenon, critically affecting national sovereignty, and also closely connected with international information flows, is the growth of unregulated financial markets along with the existence of huge pools of stateless money. 'Spurred by a spreading free-market ideology and advances in global communications', the *New York Times* reports, 'restrictions that had curbed and cosseted financial markets are being dismantled. Interest rates are being freed from government regulation. Withholding taxes are being eliminated on the foreign purchases of domestic securities. Domestic financial markets are being opened to foreigners. Financial institutions are being allowed to enter new businesses'.[14]

These measures smooth the way for a small number of very powerful transnational banking, investment and brokerage corporations to extend their activities into what were once insulated national territories. In this penetration, communication capabilities lead the way: 'Computer screens and telephones link New York almost as easily with Tokyo as with Chicago. In addition, more sophisticated investors began to look for better returns abroad'.[15]

The full consequences of these developments are still to be experienced. But already some generalizations can be made: 'As these changes gather momentum, they are gradually eroding economic boundaries, providing new opportunities for international investment *but also frustrating national economic policies* and provoking competition among the world's largest financial houses'.[16]

Huge flows of money — surplus accumulations of the transnational corporations, for the most part, as well as other hoards of wealthy individuals and businesses — move into a country, remain there for a time; but if there is a perceived threat to the principal, or a reduction in the rate of return, a frenzied withdrawal may be initiated. This, in turn, leaves the abandoned economy in a shambles. Accordingly, an economy integrated into current international financial markets increasingly becomes a hostage to the market's (capital's) reading of its economic, political and cultural internal affairs.

An episode affecting Australia illuminates the tight connections between national decisions and international finance, to the disadvantage of the former. In early 1985, Australian Prime Minister Bob Hawke departed slightly from his customary pro-USA geopolitical position and yielded to his strong domestic peace movement's demand that Australian bases not be used to monitor an MX missile test.

The financial community's reaction was immediate.

> In a few weeks, the value of the Australian dollar dropped 14 percent, to about 71 cents to the United States dollar. . . . the MX issue appeared to be the catalyst. The declining Australian dollar, the *Melbourne Age* said in an editorial, 'reflects a global loss of confidence'. . . . the MX missile crisis drew attention to Australia and cast doubt on the political strength and stability of the Hawke Government'.[17]

One important piece of information is missing in this account. Precisely *who* lost confidence in the government? Certainly not the substantial constituency in the peace movement! In fact, it was the financial and transnational corporate interests who were dismayed enough to withdraw capital and automatically put pressure on the national currency.

The flight of transnational capital, either because of fear or to chastise a national policy it disagrees with, or possibly for both reasons, has been a prominent feature of international political life in recent years. And the huge sums and flows involved make the impact of such moves highly destabilizing to the affected economy.

The victory in France of François Mitterrand and his Socialist coalition in 1981, for example, put immediate pressure on the franc and eventually forced Mitterrand to abandon whatever social measures he may have initially intended to introduce. Similar pressures have been imposed on other nations that may have attempted, however mildly, to take steps that were considered threatening to the interest of transnational capital. Abetted by the new information technologies and the instantaneous message flows they provide, transnational capital now possesses a powerful regulator of national political and economic behaviour.

The military factor

The most obvious advantage that advanced information technology offers transnational corporate business, and the few nation-states that can produce it independently, is that it allows private firms and foreign intelligence agencies to know more about another national territory, and its resources and projects, than do the leaders of that country itself. It also enables rapid and remote decision-making that may preempt domestic policy decisions. Examples of these asymmetrical relationships are numerous.

The rich possibilities, for example, that remote sensing — satellite detection of terrestial and oceanic surfaces — offers those controlling the satellite, and, not less important, the complex computer software to make best use of the satellite-sensed data, have been discussed elsewhere.[18] It is still the case, despite a few new national entrants into remote sensing activity, that the ability to use the sensed data remains a tightly controlled capability, available only to a handful of governments, their intelligence apparatuses and the big private companies that have access to the information.

Currently, the USA has a fleet of spy satellites, estimated to number about 60 at the beginning of 1983. These have been augmented recently with the launching of a still more powerful satellite by the super-secret intelligence agency, the National Reconnaissance Office (NRO).[19]

The availability of an electronic information capability that eludes national control is not limited to the skies. This seems to be the import of a cryptic account of a recent incident in Mexico:

> A United States Embassy van loaded with sophisticated electronic equipment was seized by Mexican customs agents . . . and American diplomats said . . . it was all an innocent mistake. The van, bearing diplomatic plates, was impounded with its contents after Mexican customs agents found that it had none of the necessary permits for the equipment it carried. The equipment included radio transmitters–receivers, powerful antennas, a telephone line tracer, power plants, cables and other electronic gear. . . . A spokesman for the United States Embassy . . . declined to say for what purposes the embassy was trying to import the equipment.[20]

Whatever the reason — 'innocuous', as the US Embassy personnel insisted, or not — the instrumentation possessed the capability to bypass Mexican national authority.

On a more sweeping level still, what is one to make of the news that the Belgian parliament learned about the arrival of US cruise missiles on Belgian soil *only after* the arrival? As reported, 'The timing of the first plane's arrival, about three hours after Mr Martens [the Prime Minister] told Parliament Belgium would take the missiles, *indicated aircraft carrying the weapons left the United States before Parliament learned what was happening*'.[21] In this case, the US government, and the Department of Defense in particular, were aware of the Prime Minister's decision *before* the Belgian people and their elected representatives were. This, it should be remembered, occurred in one of the most developed industrial nations in the world.

Looking beyond the event, the lesson must be deeply troubling to Europeans who are told that they will have 'full knowledge of nuclear decisions affecting their countries and [that they] would be involved in those decisions'.[22]

In fact, the nuclear 'shield' which the Pentagon holds over Western Europe and elsewhere can be seen as a means to thwart and undermine national sentiments and decisions as much as it provides protection. Actually, the control of the war-making nuclear machinery in exclusive US hands represents the ultimate in the loss of national sovereignty for the rest of the world. It signifies that the capability to protect life and property has been removed from national authority and placed elsewhere.

There are still other infringements on national sovereignty which originate with what is termed 'military necessity'. Costa Rica, for example, has national laws which prohibit the foreign ownership of radio frequencies. All the same, that country was pressed by the Reagan administration into a collaboration with the 'Voice of America', which financed the construction of a transmitter on Costa Rican soil, beamed at Nicaragua. This provocative, and essentially illegal, action was legitimized by organizing a private group inside Costa Rica to serve as the proprietary party.[23]

The international media
In the increasingly important and growing sphere of international media flows, the new instrumentation — satellites, direct satellite broadcasting, cable television, etc. — supplies the means of allowing increased access of US and a few other Western media products. These outpourings from the concentrated cultural industries in New York, Los Angeles, London and Hollywood are fed into the transmission systems of nations around the world and serve to displace national cultural creativity.

Once the facilities and installations of transmission have been set in place, the dynamics of the international marketing system — no less powerful in the cultural than in the industrial sphere — preside. These dynamics make it inevitable that the relatively inexpensive, well-crafted, commercial production of a few Western centres will prevail.

Domestic talent, artists and technicians either flock to the US studios and cultural centres or adopt locally the techniques and contents of the successful products. In either case, diversity diminishes, local creativity suffers, and transnational culture expands.

These many developments affecting economic decision-making authority, political–military autonomy and cultural creation are by no means winding down. The forces arrayed against national sovereignty, if anything, are still building. The utilization of continuously improved communication technologies, on behalf of the super-companies in the world market, is accelerating.

Promoting the process of *deregulation*, a code word for the removal of national discretion over economic activity, clears the way for transnational corporate expansion in Western Europe, Japan, Australia, Canada and most of the rest of the world.

One analysis of the emerging world telecommunications structure being established to facilitate these developments — the Integrated Services Digital Network (ISDN) — argues that 'ISDN will in actuality radically *reduce* their [less developed countries'] ability to direct and control national development. . . . ISDN incarnates only the private interests of the transnational corporations that will engineer, supply, install and make use of the emerging global grid'.[24]

The prospects

Is the nation-state moving towards oblivion? How far can these trends of transnationalization proceed? Are there any points of resistance? What may be expected in the time ahead? Can the nation-state's governing authority be transferred to the already economically prevailing super-transnational companies?

Though this last possibility is not as preposterous as it may first appear, its likelihood is not great and it certainly is not an immediate prospect. This is so because, no matter how reduced a nation-state's *economic* decision-making power becomes, as a political entity it continues to supply one indispensable function to transnational capital: it serves to maintain order in the subject territories.

It does this by a combination of means. There is increasing surveillance of the total population by a variety of sophisticated techniques, mostly employing computerization. There is the exercise of raw power — helicopter gunships patrolling restless urban areas, police forces strengthened and supplied with firepower that exceeds that of military formations in recent wars. Finally, and less centrally directed as a means of pacification, there is the commercial entertainment system, mostly television but also film, entertainment parks, shopping mall pageantry, etc. These, in their aggregate, contribute to the stupefaction of the general public.

Actually, the strong, coercive state is the inverse of the diminished welfare state. The two are bound together.

These palpable developments led one analyst to the following perspective on what the future holds:

> As the power of global corporations grows and that of nation-states declines, the rule of law will become less and less effective as a basis for the preservation of wealth. Unless and until the new global organizations assume the mantle of legitimate government, they will have to rely upon

personal loyalties and naked force to maintain order. In particular, the global corporations will form *de facto* alliances with nation states to insure the safety of their vital computer–communications networks and transportation systems. . . . The social structure of the future will be hierarchical but it will not be local in character. Wealth, power and position will be based on the ownership and control of distributed production facilities spread around the world. For this reason I have called the new system *virtual feudalism*.[25]

Whether this assessment of what will develop becomes an actuality remains to be seen. So many fragilities and instabilities exist in the international (and domestic) arena(s) that extrapolated progressions have to be approached cautiously. All the same, certain material factors are at work, and they impose their own dynamic.

However, if super-corporations are dependent on the state to provide policing power and maintain law and order against the victims of 'modernization and efficiency', the state cannot be completely written off as a failed entity. Strong coercive states have not been distinguished for their flexibility in the past. Still, there are reasons for believing that present serious problems and future disagreements between transnational capital and state authorities may open up some space for a variety of national initiatives. Some local manoeuvrability may develop, with consequences difficult to foresee at this time.

More destabilizing still to a lasting compact between transnational capital and law-and-order states is the slow but steady growth of a non-working population of working age. There is a limit to the expansion of profit-making service industries, which are expected to drain off the labour force made redundant by automation and computerization.

There are no current guidelines to indicate how this will be handled in the time to come. Also, the near-absolute dependence of transnational capital on secure global communications cannot fail to be another source of vulnerability and, possibly, disruption.

One last, but not unimportant, consideration in this admittedly schematic review must be taken into account: the people. The late nineteenth- and early twentieth-century expectations (of some) of an aroused proletariat, shaking off its shackles, may not be applicable in the information-using era. But the distance from propertyless, sweated industrial labour to the open-shirted information worker may not be as great or as unbridgeable as the information age enthusiasts proclaim. And then, there are the growing number who never find jobs.

In any case, it seems premature to abandon the idea of social struggle, however different the social terrain may now be. Significant commonalities remain between the underpinnings of industrial and transnational capital.

While the reasons for the growing conflict between national sovereignty and transnational capital are tangible and very real indeed, some see the antagonism in semantic or personal terms.

In the semantic approach, current developments that are destroying national decision-making are seen as necessary steps towards the state of 'interdependence', which is now supposed to exist between nations. According to this interpretation, all nations have to give up something in order to contribute to the general well-being of the entire community of nation-states. They are all 'interdependent'. But, as the saying goes, some are more interdependent than others. Most often, what is called interdependence is, in fact, a situation of unequal power, in which one state imposes its will on others or another. The more influential state, as could be expected, also possesses the cultural/communication authority to define the unequal relationship as one of 'interdependence'.

The personalized approach describes those who insist on the importance of national sovereignty as being 'overly emotional'. For example, 'I do not wish to deny the validity of concerns about sovereignty, but one of the greatest dangers today, as we see growing volumes of transborder data flows, is headlong progress down this emotional line of thinking'. Again, 'there is a tendency for "sovereignty" to become an emotionally-charged word; there is fertile ground for rhetoric and there are dangers of over-reaction'.[26]

It is difficult to accept that the 'greatest danger today' is excess emotionality over national sovereignty. More important, by far, is the unchecked advance of the power of transnational capital. Perhaps there hasn't been enough passion and rhetoric? Perhaps not enough people have been made aware about what is happening to social existence everywhere by the activities of unaccountable transnational capital.

The conclusion here, at least, is that every assistance should be given to raising both the analytical and the emotional level of as many people as possible, so that they may engage clear-headedly in defence of their own, and the general, economic well-being, political independence, and cultural diversity and creativity.

Notes

1. 'International Information Flow: A Plan for Action', *Business Roundtable* (New York), January 1985:9–10.

2. David E. Sanger, 'New Old-hand at IBM Helm', *New York Times*, 29 January 1985.

3. *Business Roundtable*, January 1985:6–11.

4. *ibid.*

5. *ibid.*

6. Walter B. Wriston, 'Policy Formation for the Global Market Place', *Chronicle of International Communication*, 1985, VI(1): 1, 7.

7. *ibid.*

8. *Business Roundtable*, January 1985:6.

9. Gary Putka, 'Strong Dollar Has Led US Firms to Transfer Production Oversea', *Wall Street Journal*, 9 April 1985.

10. Barry Newman, 'Single-country Unions of Europe Try to Cope with Multinationals', *Wall Street Journal*, 30 November 1983.

11. *ibid.*

12. *Business Roundtable*, January 1985:10–11 (emphasis added).

13. 'A Delivery That May Be Dresser-France's Last', *Business Week*, 18 October 1982.

14. Nicholas D. Kristof, 'World Financial Curbs Eased by Technology and Ideology', *New York Times*, 26 January 1985.

15. *ibid.*

16. *ibid.* (emphasis added).

17. Steve Lohr, 'Australians' MX Stand Isn't Popular', *New York Times*, 24 February 1985.

18. Herbert I. Schiller, *Who Knows: Information in the Age of the Fortune 500*. Norwood, NJ: Ablex Publishing, 1981. See especially chapter 6, 'Planetary Resource Information Flows: A New Dimension of Hegemonic Power or Global Social Utility?'

19. James Bamford, 'America's Supersecret Eyes in Space', *New York Times Sunday Magazine*, 13 January 1985.

20. Richard J. Meislin, 'Mexico Seizes US Van; Mistake Envoys Say', *New York Times*, 10 April 1985.

21. 'Belgium Says Missiles Are Now Operational', *New York Times*, 17 March (emphasis added).

22. Leslie H. Gelb, 'US Tries to Fight Allied Resistance to Nuclear Arms', *New York Times*, 14 February 1985.

23. Caitlin Randall, 'Voice of America Takes on Nicaraguan Radio', *Electronic Media*, 13 December 1984.

24. Dan Schiller, 'The Emerging Global Grid: Planning for What?' *Media, Culture and Society*, 1985, 7(1):105–6.

25. Abbe Moshowitz, 'The Future with AI: Freedom and Community?' Paper prepared for the Office of Technology Assessment, US Congress Joint Workshop on 'Societal Impacts of Artificial Intelligence', 9 November 1984, pp. 10–11.

26. Peter Robinson, 'Sovereignty and Data: Some Perspectives'. Paper presented to the conference on 'The Information Economy: Its Implications for Canada's Industrial Strategy', sponsored by the Royal Society of Canada and the University of Toronto/University of Waterloo Cooperative on Information Technology, 30 May–1 June 1984, pp. 1–2.

3

Communication satellites and the Third World

Donna A. Demac

According to Greek mythology, the gods lived on Olympus. Each had distinctive powers and appetites. Zeus, the supreme deity, threw thunderbolts in jealous rage; Orion, the beautiful but hot-headed young hunter, declared vengeance on a king; Aphrodite, the goddess of beauty, beguiled all. Yet the gods could also be compassionate. Cooperation and intense rivalry went on simultaneously.

Much the same could be said about the nations that are making use of the main orbit around the earth through which messages are transmitted from one part of the globe to another — the geostationary orbit (GSO). Here, 22,300 miles from the earth, in the plane of the equator, is the only orbit in which communication satellites maintain a fixed position relative to points below and are capable of providing continuous transmission to up to one-third of the earth's surface.

Nations have been engaged in cooperative and competitive activity in the GSO for more than twenty years. Many are the pursuits — and vast the potential benefits — made possible by satellite technology. It embodies an unprecedented amount of human knowledge and is at the forefront of a process of change that is affecting the scientific, cultural and commercial environments of all nations.

Space is no longer the vast and unknown frontier it once was. There are over 130 satellites in the GSO that are being used for broadcast and telephone communication, remote sensing, data transmission and military activities. This number could double by 1990. Most satellites are owned by a handful of developed nations, primarily the USA and the Soviet Union, joined by the Western European countries and Japan.

In the developing world, India, Indonesia, Brazil, China and Mexico own satellites. Many more countries lease transmission from one of the common-user organizations. Intelsat is a cooperatively owned system with 110 national members, serving 170 countries. Other common-user systems include Intersputnik, Arabsat and Palapa, which is owned by Indonesia.

The costs of building, launching and maintaining satellite networks are enormous. For this reason, bilateral and multilateral participation have turned out to be advantageous at every stage, from manufacture to launching. Joint ventures are typical; single-country systems, from conception to operation in orbit, are extremely rare. This suggests the great importance of an environment that enables many different interests to be developed by the occupants of modern-day Olympus.

Satellites and developing nations
The importance of satellites for the developing world has grown owing to the deteriorating economic conditions in many countries. Unfortunately, there has been little change in the sharp contrast between the abundance of telecommunications networks in parts of the industrialized world and the lack of basic communications technology in most of the developing world.

A 1984 study by the International Telecommunication Union (ITU), entitled *The Missing Link*, found that there are approximately 600 million telephones in the world. None the less, two-thirds of the world's population have no access to a telephone. There are more telephones in Tokyo than on the entire African continent. This study recommended increased emphasis on telecommunications in the developing world and said that a sustained global commitment, amounting to some US 12 billion dollars annually, would be necessary to put every person within reach of a telephone by the year 2000.[1]

Until recently, little research had been done on the economic and social benefits of telecommunications, but studies carried out by the World Bank, the Organization for Economic Cooperation and Development (OECD) and others have concluded that the benefit–cost ratio of telecommunications investments in developing countries can run as high as 100 to 1.[2]

High technology in the 1980s is a combination of computer hardware and software, robotics, fibre optics and other equipment. Yet satellites can be particularly important in a country's effort to establish basic telephone connections, leading in turn to improved medical and emergency care, communication between the town centre and remote areas, and increased commercial activity.[3]

Most of the population in the developing world is situated in small agricultural communities. It is estimated that 87 percent of the world's population is outside the range of urban communication and transportation facilities. Since the dispersion of satellite transmission provides for distribution within the coverage or 'footprint' area, any location can be reached as long as it is within the footprint. Many people in these countries live in locations that are costly to reach by traditional, terrestrial lines or ocean cables, whereas satellite transmission is insensitive to terrain and can penetrate deserts, jungles, mountains or Arctic outposts with no additional cost or loss of power.

Much of the developing world approaches the communications challenge with no existing system in place. A fairly comprehensive satellite-based system can be developed in a period of five to ten years, whereas a comparable terrestrial system would take much longer. Finally, the cost of a broadcast satellite increases relatively slowly with the size of the area to be served, while the cost of a terrestrial network increases proportionately to the region served.

In spite of the possible long-term advantages in the use of satellites, few developing nations are in a position to expand their technological base significantly at this time. Most developing countries lack the funds to launch a satellite. Institutional barriers, more immediate priorities and the lack of an overall technical orientation create additional obstacles.

While certain decisions can be postponed, there exist important developments that no nation can afford to ignore, as they will directly bear upon the possibility of access to satellite technology and other telecommunications facilities. These developments include the controversy over the distribution of orbital positions in the GSO and the decisive move on the part of several nations in the direction of making market-place competition the dominant Muse of the GSO.

Entering the ring
Twenty years ago, outer space was declared the common heritage of mankind. An international treaty stated that the space environment and its resources are to be used 'for the benefit and in the interests of all countries . . . and shall be the province of all mankind'. The GSO is not available for national appropriation. The frequencies and orbital slots necessary for satellites to function cannot be owned. This principle drew little attention as long as only a few countries were involved in space activities. Over the last decade, however, many more countries have become interested in the potential benefits from satellites.

As awareness of the value of geostationary satellites has grown, use of the natural resources linked to satellites — the GSO and associated frequencies — has also increased. These are limited natural resources. Technical inventions, including more powerful satellite antennas and closer spacing between satellites, have offered new ways of maximizing use of GSO. This is not sufficient, however, to ease the concerns of many nations, especially in the developing world, over the possibility that certain parts of the GSO could be filled up in the future.

A space rush is therefore taking place. Over a very short time there has been a marked increase in the number of launchings, though the number of countries owning satellites has not grown significantly.

Approximately 48 of the 80 communication satellites in the GSO in mid-1985 had been launched since 1979; in the same time period, only India and Brazil became satellite-owning countries. The possibility that a small part of the GSO at certain frequencies could be exhausted before long has been noted by congressional and Federal Communications Commission (FCC) reports. These agencies see a solution to the problem of congestion in the use of advanced satellite technologies and new frequency-reuse techniques. But to many developing countries a plan is needed that partitions the resource and allocates slots to each nation in advance.

The International Telecommunication Union

The regulation of the use of spectrum resources is carried out by the International Telecommunication Union (ITU), a United Nations agency. For most of its existence, the ITU has been a technical organization with a mandate to coordinate and research frequency usage over a broad range of radio, microwave, maritime and, most recently, satellite technologies.[4]

Orbital positions have been given on a first-come, first-served basis. The procedure involves the recording of a satellite's frequency assignment, orbital position and relevant operating characteristics in the Master International Frequency Register. Such registry entitles the assignment to 'international recognition and protection against harmful interference'. This includes protection against harmful interference from those coming later.

There are few examples where a 'latecomer' has encountered problems in obtaining its desired orbit position. India and Indonesia had to alter their initial registrations in the late 1970s. India, in particular, claims that this entailed considerable expense. These examples, while not numerous, reinforce the notion of the need for a new way of distributing orbital slots.

In 1979 the surge in favour of change resulted in a vote, carried by the two-thirds membership in the ITU from developing countries, requiring the Union to hold two conferences in the 1980s to consider the principles and possible planning methods necessary to bring about 'equitable access in practice' to the GSO. This event should be seen in the context of debates that were also taking place concerning a New International Economic Order and a New World Information and Communication Order.

A coalescing of forces had occurred that included an awareness on the part of many developing countries of the limits of the trickle-down theory of development: a fear of the power of foreign media — especially satellite-transmitted entertainment programmes — to disrupt longstanding customs, and the knowledge that information and communications resources were of immense social and commercial importance. The MacBride Commission report had stated: 'There can be no genuine, effective independence without the communication resources needed to safeguard it.' The 1979 ITU vote reflected a strong conviction that ground rules for sharing the GSO were needed if all countries were to be empowered to use this resource independently.

The space WARC

The first of the World Administrative Radio Conferences (WARCs) stipulated in the 1979 resolution was held in Geneva in August 1985.[5] It lasted nearly six weeks and was attended by 110 of the 160 ITU member-nations. The second WARC will take place in 1988 to see to the implementation of decisions made in 1985.

Delegates attending the 1985 WARC considered many different proposals for planning principles and methods to achieve equitable access. The issue of orbital allotment came down to the conflict between two different views of how to maximize access to the GSO. The USA and UK, the countries that were most opposed to *a priori* planning, were also the ones that had made the most dramatic push towards deregulation and privatization. Most of the other developed countries opposed orbital reservations, though Canada, Australia and Japan were receptive to certain mixed planning approaches that would provide *a priori* plans for a limited part of the orbit and designated frequencies.

Other countries proposed long-term reservations, ranging from seven years to indefinite assignments. Stanley Malumbe, head of the Kenyan delegation, described the existing distribution procedure as 'indiscriminate and catastrophic' and said that planning was the only effective way to establish an access guarantee. The conviction that changes in procedures would not alter the essentially unbridled activity of the industrialized world at the expense of the developing nations was evident throughout.

Yet, though the issue of a guarantee was the centre of gravity, it was only one of a number of important considerations. Many delegates were at least as concerned about sharing information and developing negotiating strategies as they were about spectrum issues. The demand that every country have a guaranteed slot and frequencies was linked to demonstrating future-oriented national development plans as well as the ability to function effectively within the ITU. Moreover, beyond the conference lay many possible contracts for assessing the cost and feasibility of a host of telecommunications systems as well as business deals for the provision of services by outside vendors. The conference afforded many opportunities for delegates to discuss regional and bilateral transactions.

Because there were few reporters at the conference, the reports that reached the public failed to record significant differences between the 1979 and 1985 conferences. Principally, several developing nations, including China, Brazil and Mexico, had become satellite-owning states. This meant that they were concerned about protecting existing satellites. Their change in emphasis complicated efforts to build coalitions around *a priori* proposals that could require the modification of existing allotments.

For example, China's position, which called for no reservations but for changes in procedures, was very close to that of the USA. This was particularly noteworthy in light of China's plan to launch three additional satellites before long. Delegate Chen Zhongging said that his country might have to enter into negotiations with as many as four countries: the Soviet Union, India, Indonesia and Japan. At the same time, the developed countries mentioned above were more sympathetic to the need for some accommodation of developing country demands.

The only time that an *a priori* plan had been adopted was at the 1977 broadcasting satellite conference in which orbital positions were awarded for every country in Europe, Africa and Asia. At that time the USA prevented the plan from extending to North and South America; a broadcast satellite plan was adopted for the Western Hemisphere in 1983.

By 1985 many countries had expressed dissatisfaction with the 1977 plan and were more aware that planning absent mechanisms that permitted adjustment could impede the use of technologies based on up-to-date technical efficiencies and orbit usage. This was a note of caution, one that led to a revision of some of the very impassioned positions that had been taken in 1979.

Furthermore, developing countries wrestled with the question of how advances in satellite technology would affect them. One of the arguments of the countries opposed to any reservation scheme was that technical improvements made planning unnecessary. Yet this argument was often resisted on the grounds that less affluent countries might not be able to afford the most advanced technologies and, in fact, had found the price of yesterday's technology prohibitive. India's proposals emphasized this by calling for an orbital plan that was based on 'feasible, applicable and suitable technologies'.

This position — that a plan be practical for all — was a thorny one. It is essentially an extension of a change made in the ITU Convention in 1982 which said the ITU should take into account 'the special needs of the developing countries and the geographical situation of particular countries'. Some developed countries regard this as a demand by the developing nations for a 'free lunch', or as a demand for inequality through preferences in favour of the developing world. The developing countries, on the other hand, often describe this call for attention to their 'special needs' as an effort to institute greater balance in use of the orbit/spectrum resource.

The fact that this disagreement did not result in a confrontation is a clear indication of the importance that countries of all viewpoints attached to stable regulation of the GSO. And, at the end of a long and difficult five and a half weeks, when many delegates had already gone home, those remaining reached an agreement that was a combination of the approaches that had initially been presented.

A limited *a priori* reservation scheme was adopted that should permit each country to satisfy requirements for national services from at least one orbital position, within a predetermined portion of the GSO and predetermined frequency bands. For those frequencies and orbital positions not subject to *a priori* planning, improvements are to be made in ITU procedures that, theoretically, will ensure prompt attention to the requirements of latecomer nations.

In addition, planning is to take account of the needs of multi-administration systems, such as Intelsat and Intersputnik, in order to enable them to continue to meet the needs of countries for international and domestic services. (The importance of changing policies towards Intelsat is discussed below.)

The conference outcome was, on the one hand, a compromise reached after the final hour. On the other hand, it could be seen as a genuine step forward for the developing nations. Differences in countries' positions before the conference seem to have affected their sentiments about what it achieved. *South*, a magazine about the Third World, reported that the adoption of a plan that would reserve orbital positions and allow countries to have an exclusive claim on a limited number of unused frequencies had allayed Third World concerns about being squeezed out of the space resources race.[6] In contrast, statements made after the WARC by the US State Department indicated its dissatisfaction that the conference had been too 'political'.

The WARC results are clearly in need of much elaboration before they can be seen as providing an institutionally enforceable access guarantee. The agreements reached at the end of the 1985 conference will be finalized at a second conference in 1988. In the meantime, many tasks must be completed which were specified at the end of the 1985 conference.

One of the most important inter-session tasks involves developing a software package that could be used by the 1988 conference attendees in the preparation of the final orbit allotment plan.

Planning exercises will have to be carried out in advance to determine whether all variables pertaining to geographic locations and frequency interference have been included, and to test the software's flexibility. For this to be adequate, countries will need to determine more exactly what their needs are for satellite transmission. This includes ascertaining the desirability of options for regional or sub-regional satellite systems and the optimal frequencies necessary for such service. One could thus add an additional element to the maxim, 'access is process', to say that, in the context of satellite orbit planning, 'access is process *and* research'. During the inter-session period nations may enter a new stage of negotiation, one that adheres even more to practical realities.[7]

Competition in orbit
In the 1960s the USA chose Apollo, the god of light and truth, as the symbol of its space programme; twenty years later it has moved on to Hermes, the god of commerce. This, it would seem, is part of a plan to open up young markets, including the telecommunications markets in developing countries, and to accelerate the introduction of new technologies. But competition-above-all also fits in with the emphasis on privatization in a growing number of countries, including the USA, countries of Western Europe and even Third World nations such as Brazil.

The most dramatic initiative in the satellite field has involved the decision by the US government to endorse competition with Intelsat by companies seeking to compete in the international provision of satellite services.[8]

In the autumn of 1985, the applications of six companies were conditionally approved by the Federal Communications Commission.[9] The FCC decision stated that they would all be prohibited from entering into the public switched telephone networks that provide the bulk of Intelsat's business. None the less, this action is of great importance to the satellite plans of other nations owing to the potentially negative impact of these new systems on the pricing of Intelsat services, which, up until now, has been geared towards providing services to developing as well as industrialized countries.

Additionally, a very large number of new channels were authorized by this one action — amounting to only a portion of the new satellite systems recently authorized by the FCC that will provide overseas transmission. The vast scope of these satellites' 'footprints' also indicates their likely importance to the social and political life of many developing nations.

A brief description of each of these applications will serve to reinforce their importance. The six companies involved include

Orion Satellite Corporation, International Satellite Inc. (ISI), RCA American Communications, Cygnus Satellite Corporation, Pan American Satellite Corporation (PanamSat), and Financial Satellite Corporation (Finansat).

Orion's plan consists of two satellites, each with 22 transponders, or 'channels', which would provide video, data and audio services, on a condominium basis, to large corporate users in North America and Western Europe. ISI's system would have two in-orbit satellites, each with 32 transponders, providing video, audio and data services throughout the continental USA and to the western portion of Europe as far as the Adriatic Sea.

RCA's proposed system would use six transponders of its previously authorized SATCOM VI domestic satellite. These would be capable of reaching Europe and Africa with a range of video and data services. The fourth company, Cygnus, would have two satellites, with 16 transponders each. They would transmit data and video to the Caribbean Basin, Puerto Rico, the US Virgin Islands and portions of Central America, as well as to Western Europe and the USA.

Panamsat has proposed to use only one satellite, with 36 transponders, to relay international traffic between North and South America and domestic services in South America. Finally, Finansat proposed two in-orbit satellites, with 24 transponders each, to be used to link networks between the Atlantic and Pacific regions.

This comes to a grand total of 230 new channels of satellite transmission!

The FCC explained its decision by calling upon the reigning Muse of Washington: Competition. In a section of its decision titled 'General Policy Considerations', it said:

> The Executive branch states that 'advocating and adopting international communications policies which stress reliance on free enterprise, competition and free trade' are policies necessary to further the US goal of promotion of competition and reliance on market forces. . . . The hallmark of a competitive market is the maximization of customer choice which can be effectuated by allowing multiple entrants.

Specifically regarding the developing countries, the Commission acknowledged that providing satellite service to these nations was a significant goal in the original creation of a global system and the reason that Intelsat has charged uniform rates for its services. The possibility that Intelsat's rates might rise because of the authorization of systems intending to compete along major Intelsat routes was dismissed as unlikely, owing to anticipated market expansion.

There remain a number of unanswered questions, in addition to the validity of the FCC's predictions regarding the telecommunications market-place. These questions, which also apply to similar ventures in other countries, include:

1. Does the surge of commercial activity imply a drain of capital away from Europe and developing countries into the USA? (A number of European countries are preparing to market services abroad and have thus far refused to sign with any of the previously-named companies.)

2. Is unlimited competition required to produce the highest cost efficiencies?

3. What commitment do the private investors have to global connectivity?

4. What signs are there that private interests will offer affordable rates to developing countries? Will present changes in the market-place cause the price of satellite services to rise beyond what is affordable for developing countries now seeking to improve their telecommunications infrastructures?

5. What is the risk of bankruptcy, and what impact would this have on the overall economic climate for international telecommunications services?

Trade and business opportunities and network efficiencies are not equivalent for countries that are still attempting to establish the basic tools for participating in international transactions. If satellite services are approached strictly on a commercial basis, this may have an adverse impact on access to technologies and services by the less affluent nations. Moreover, much is known today about the pitfalls of branch-plant economies and trade relations that concentrate on only a handful of nations. The present effort by a few countries to develop the private satellite sector to penetrate on a global basis may not augur well for nations which may have little to gain in terms of trade that would serve national development objectives. None the less, parts of the developing world have been targeted as the largest potential markets for satellite and other telecommunications services.

At the present time, one can see a battle of immeasurable social and economic consequence unfolding in relation to the geostationary orbit. The more than twenty-year history of international cooperation and competition in the satellite field is surely relevant. Many joint ventures are proceeding apace. Yet the space age has reached a period of momentous transition. Many developing countries are staking their claim to the orbit/spectrum resource by demanding changes in the basic principles and procedures that have governed use of the GSO. At the same time, there is an aggressive push towards market-place 'regulation' taking place which challenges the basis of global participation in another, but no less basic, way.

As satellite activities are pursued by more nations, there is a clear need for broad-based consideration of the multitude of interest to be accommodated. The ITU is the most likely forum for this purpose. The WARCs of the 1980s could result in the adoption of a more effective reconciliation between the commercial objectives of the space 'have' states and the need-oriented goals of the developing world. However, the ascendancy of the competitive Muse is a sign of diminished interest in international accommodation by some few nations. Obviously, future negotiating positions will need to bridge the issues of equitable access to the GSO and the commercialization of outer space in a more sophisticated fashion than has been required in the past.[10]

Herein lies the challenge for countries seeking to establish their role in the Olympian orbit and to make international communication a participatory reality.

Notes

1. International Telecommunication Union, *The Missing Link*. Report of the Independent Commission for Worldwide Telecommunications Development, 1984.

2. International Telecommunication Union, *Telecommunications for Development*. Study by OECD and ITU, 1983. See also R. Saunders, J. Warford and B. Wellenius, *Telecommunications for Economic Development*. Washington: World Bank, 1983.

3. Numerous examples are provided in E. Hudson, *When Telephones Reach the Village: The Role of Telecommunications in Rural Development*. Norwood, NJ: Ablex Publishing, 1984.

4. G. Codding Jr. and A. Rutkonski, *The International Telecommunication Union in a Changing World*. Dedham: Artech House, 1983.

5. For background to the 1985 Space WARC see D. Demac, G. Codding, H. Hudson and R. Jakhu, *Equity in Orbit: The 1985 ITU Space WARC*. London: International Institute of Communications, 1985.

6. *South*, November 1985, p. 151.

7. See n. 5.

8. See W. Dizard Jr, 'Policy Issues and Telecommunications', and R. Colino, 'INTELSAT: Facing the World of Tomorrow', both in *Journal of International Affairs*, Summer 1985.

9. 'In the Matter of Establishment of Satellite Systems Providing International Communications', FCC Docket no. 84–1299, released 25 July 1985.

10. D. Demac (ed.), *Tracing New Orbits: Cooperation and Competition in International Satellite Development*. New York: Columbia University Press, 1986.

4

The social implications of technological innovations in communication

James D. Halloran

We need the knowledge that only research can provide before we can develop adequate communication policies.

Proposals for an International Programme of Communication Research   Unesco, Paris, 1971

Mass communication research was established and developed primarily as a response to the perceived needs of the media industries. In a commercial setting, where advertising revenue was all important, it was considered necessary to have detailed information about the size, composition, predisposition and reactions of readers, listeners and viewers. This was service or administrative research — essentially atheoretical, which had the clear purpose of serving the media. The problems or issues were defined from a media standpoint, and both research questions and research methodologies were formulated and operationalized within these relatively narrow media-oriented parameters.

This 'media centredness' continued to prevail even when, from entirely different angles, concern was expressed about the possible detrimental effects of the media, usually with regard to violence, sex, political bias and trivialization. These 'problems', and the research which attempted to address them, tended to be expressed in terms of what the media were doing to people rather than in terms of what people with different experiences, opportunities, skills and competences were making of what the media provided. Even a shift in direction from media as scapegoat to media as panacea (education) did not fundamentally change this line of thought, which showed no understanding of institutional relationships, the communication process, social structure or the wider social context.

'Communication policies' was not a term that was widely used. Of course, there were policies, but these tended to be latent and fragmented rather than overt and articulated. Moreover, as already indicated, the research that served these policies was rarely expressed or seen as having such a role. Its real function was hidden under the cloak of 'science', that is, value-free positivism.

However, from the mid-1960s onwards it was possible to detect a fundamentally different approach to the study of the media and the communication process. Central to this approach, which was by no means homogeneous, was an holistic, sociological, contextual standpoint which saw the media not in isolation, but in relation to other institutions and processes. This facilitated a critical orientation so that research might now attempt to serve society rather than the media. The two — society and the media — were no longer equated as they had often been, albeit implicitly, in the past, and the emphasis shifted to *communication needs*, and to how these might be best served by media policies and practices.

This critical, holistic approach, with its emphasis on social needs rather than media requirements, underpins what follows on the possible implications of technological developments in communication — one of our main concerns for the future. But whatever we think of the case presented in these pages, we must remember that it represents a shift in quality rather than quantity. Most 'research' is still commissioned to serve the system. Much remains to be done.

The main focus of this chapter is on the social implications (in the widest sense of the term) of the introduction and application of communication technologies. As research that addresses itself *directly* to this question is rather thin on the ground, an attempt will be made to draw on the results from research and studies in related areas, in order to evaluate the contemporary situation and suggest some guidelines and possibilities for future research.

A basic assumption in the approach adopted here is that the application of the technologies and associated institutional and organizational changes will be governed by a range of factors, including political and economic considerations, which may or may not be related to individual or societal perceptions of *communication needs*. The mode of application and the rates of development — domestic and business, individual and societal — will differ from country to country, from innovation to innovation, and from institution to institution. Estimates of these rates are available in some countries, and provide indications of possibilities, policies and plans. These, together with other factors covered in the course of this chapter, should offer some guidelines for research developments.

Another basic assumption is that the innovations and changes do not occur in isolation; they need to be examined within the wider social context, and in the light of current social trends. Obviously, these contexts and trends will differ from country to country. For example, the analysis of social trends in some industrialized societies, say, with particular reference to the family (this is just one example) and the possibility of the closer integration of the domestic unit into communication networks, has indicated that developments in communication over the next decade must be studied within the wider social context and in relation to trends of the kind which will now be discussed — tentative, speculative and incomplete though these are.

First, let us consider the movement of work, or certain aspects of it, away from the conventional work-place, so that it is no longer confined inside specific time/space frameworks, as in the past. With this change, and the development of work in the home, some degree of overlap may occur between compulsory working time and what hitherto has generally been regarded as free time within the same space. In families where this takes place, there would no longer be a clear break between work in the home and outside work. Of course, there are families and families and the implications will be different in different classes and social groupings. For example, certain groups — usually relatively elite groups — already rely for vital 'work' information and communication exchanges on business lunches, cocktail parties, entertainment in the home, weekend social and sporting occasions and so on.

Second, we might ask if there are some indications of the beginning of the end of the school's monopoly of education — a change which might possibly lead to the development of a widespread phenomenon of self-education, and a genuine 'continuing education' for which the family (again, certain types of family) could assume responsibility.

Signs of the gradual reduction of investment and involvement by the state in the social sector (health, housing, amenities and education), and the end of the concept of public and social services, as some of us have come to know it over the past half-century, have been detected. In fact, in some countries deliberate policies in this connection are being vigorously pursued. Where such trends develop, people might be forced to consider the possibility of finding new ways of managing social relationships, where the emphasis could be on self-organization, self-supervision and the development of voluntary work and mutual aid systems, based on associative relationships and organizations.

The decline of party politics as we have known it in many countries, and the development of referenda on specific issues and/or in selected areas, 'Community Chest politics', decentralization and the growth of pressure groups is another trend which could be relevant for our work.

In some places there has been a change in emphasis from productivity to distribution and sales promotion, and this has been accompanied by a change from mass advertising to more specific targeted advertising, and by an increasing diversification of goods corresponding to a fragmentation of the consumer population.

A growing tendency to question the conventional work/leisure opposition mythologies has been noted. There is some evidence to suggest that a reduction in compulsory working time (this seems inevitable, for one reason or another) has never yet resulted in increased leisure for the groups which are not included in formal work. The lot of some women in Western industrial societies might illustrate this, in that non-working women have been said to have no real leisure because leisure cannot exist without work. It has been suggested that the belief that change and freedom can be achieved through leisure, as conventionally defined, *in opposition to work* is mistaken. Leisure itself can become an interesting activity, with a creative cultural and social dimension, only if it stems from, is an extension of, is complementary to and is essentially related to, the main social activity, which is work.

It has also been suggested that there is a decline not only in the influence of the protestant work ethic, but also in the influence of its successor, the materialistic work ethic. The expressive work ethic, or even the non-work ethic, may have taken over, particularly with younger people who are also said to be more sceptical, questioning of authority, pessimistic, and even despondent as to what the future holds for them. But the evidence is conflicting here, and there are clear differences in attitude, both within and between societies.

It needs to be emphasized that the points above simply refer to some social trends which it has been suggested might possibly apply to a greater or lesser degree in most industrialized societies. They should be seen as examples of some of the things we should consider in what is essentially an holistic approach to research. The list is certainly not exhaustive.

It should also be noted that, if there are differences within industrialized societies — and there are — then obviously there are likely to be greater differences between these societies and those in the Third World, although it should not be assumed that all these 'trend issues', particularly when suitably adjusted and adapted, are irrelevant in the Third World.

One of the main preliminary tasks in any comparative research exercise would be to identify, analyse and interpret the relevant social trends in each of the countries being studied in relation to which communication development would then be examined and its implications assessed. The family offers a suitable focus for this type of research, and it is used here for illustrative purposes; but, needless to say, there could be other foci.

These points are made here to provide illustrations of questions that might be asked in research and, above all, to emphasize again that innovations and developments in communication, and the implications of these, should be studied not in isolation, but in relation to other social processes and institutions. *A systematic analysis of these processes and institutions should be provided for each country where research is carried out.*

Within this wider context of social trends and developments, we must attempt to list communication issues and problems which call for research. These issues, focusing on the quality of life and the implications of technological development in communication, reflect a critical, policy-oriented approach to the subject.

If one accepts the general principle that underlies the relevance of the social trends argument outlined above, some of the functions of the new media technology with regard to the family may be seen as follows.

Updating of knowledge. This might be at the expense of leisure time, particularly with regard to the logic and language of the computer. The first stage in the penetration of the family in this way, in free time, by micro-electronics is alleged to be in the shape of recreation and creativity. But what recreation and creativity? It may be that these technological initiatives, these forms of family penetration, simply wear the mask of creativity, and are little more than marketing manoeuvres which reinforce the dominance of the production rationale.

The educational function. This is somewhat different from the updating function. It has to do with the extension of the role of the school into the family unit, possibly reinforcing the importance and the autonomy of the family unit by restoring to it some of the responsibilities confiscated by schools at the parents' expense. The parents might well become full educators again, with all that this means in terms of socialization.

The displacement function. This could apply both to 'old' media and temporal factors, that is, changes in patterns of media use made possible by the increased flexibility of the new technology, for example video recording.

The mobilization function. The media could be used to facilitate various forms of social interaction, for instance with regard to the activities of housewives in suburbia through, say, the setting up of information networks at a local level. These might facilitate participation in community affairs, and lead to active rather than passive use of the media.

Overall, the following questions might be put to the test:

1. Will the computerization of leisure and the new methods of communication lead the family to retire within itself, to increasing privatization and to the reinforcement of the isolation and anonymity increasingly experienced in big urban housing estates?

2. Will the availability of the new media technology lead to more real choice, to increased creativity, autonomy and participation, or will it reinforce the reliance on commerce and cultural production — the creation of needs which can be met by increased production?

Present indications, such as they are, taken together with predictions based on past related experience, suggest that the new media technology is likely to be introduced in such a way as to reinforce the old. But — and this is important — the opportunities and possibilities for creative use are unevenly distributed between the social classes.

Attention, then, must be given to the existence of differential opportunities, to different patterns of provision and use, and to the consequences of these differences in different groups and classes, within any given country, and between countries at different stages of development. Moreover, in examining these different possibilities, opportunities and uses, we need to go beyond simple time-budget approaches to more qualitative appreciations of how free time is used, and to give consideration to the different implications at different levels in society.

We must take note of what has been called 'the alienation of time'. In simple terms, this relates to the 'time spent waiting' by the underprivileged and the facilities and opportunities of the privileged which make possible the optimum use of time. Put crudely, the former not only wait and queue, but also are more inclined to the passive consumption of television and other institutional services provided. The privileged have much more freedom to organize themselves, and they use their time accordingly. They have more facilities, more scope, and therefore definitely save time. In this connection it is worth noting that research indicates that members of the dominant class are increasingly becoming people who are always busy, especially during their leisure time (see earlier comments). They cannot allow themselves to waste their time, which is increasingly devoted to accumulating 'social capital' (having as many social contacts as possible at one's disposal), with the accompanying 'cultural capital' and the building up of social power.

The privileged in society are those who have extremely socialized leisure and recreational habits, and who are least subjected to the consumption of mass media. One of the main questions is whether the introduction of the new media technology into the home, by reducing participation in social relations and physical encounters, will primarily affect those who are currently most under the influence of television and radio. Again, we see the importance of the overlap between occupation and leisure — considerable overlap in one case, but in the other an apparently unbridgeable gap between the two.

The introduction of highly individualized, even individualistic, electronic games into the home may also have important implications. They may even contribute to family disintegration; for, although they may be conducive to the increased presence of all members in the home at the same time, 'togetherness' in this sense is not the same as communication. It has also been suggested that women will experience difficulty in, or not have the same opportunities as men for, adapting to these new techniques.

As already indicated, the research which speaks directly to our central theme does not take us very far. Still, what there is must be identified and taken into account, if only to help us to avoid the mistakes of the past. So let us begin by attempting to categorize the embryonic research in this general area, being very generous as to what we include, but without any attempt at comprehensiveness.

Research on social implications to date
First, although not necessarily foremost, there are some psychological–experimental studies, mainly in the USA, on various aspects of human–machine interaction. At an entirely different level, particularly in Latin America, there is an ever-increasing number of attempts to explore the potential of the new technology for health, social, education, community and democratic purposes. On the other hand, head- and nose-counting die hard, and in several countries there is no shortage of quantitative, descriptive studies which attempt to measure and classify the availability and the users/subscribers of different services (such as teletext). Closely related to this type of work are the attempts to look into the future and to forecast demand for, and the possible utilization of, the different innovations. These are the worlds of 'units', 'consumers', 'purchasers', 'adopters', 'rejectors' and so on, where 'human beings', 'people', 'families' and 'homes' are in danger of becoming merely terms of historical interest.

Social impact research is not entirely ignored, but what little there is tends to be very narrowly conceived, and confined somewhat unrealistically to a single medium or innovation. Information society studies, such as those in France, although lacking sociological refinement, are more holistic in conception, but, not surprisingly, they have a long way to go before they can provide us with answers to the questions we raise.

Some studies of the international implications of technological developments are more challenging, but are often circumscribed by the size and complexity of the subject matter. This has led to criticism that they tend to verge on the journalistic and the speculative. Not that this should surprise us, for the general field boasts a plethora of speculative studies, with prognostications which range from doom and damnation to Utopia and universality.

Speculations apart, an overview of the several attempts to get to grips with the problem tends to produce a depressing feeling of *déjà vu*. For, on the whole, much of the research just mentioned (some of the socially purposive work being a notable exception) tends to be marked by the same inadequacies which have characterized mainstream and conventional mass communication research over the past thirty years. It is important that these inadequacies (and, where possible, the factors which create and sustain them) should be identified, for they need to be recognized and countered before a truly critical research programme can be formulated.

At the heart of the problem are the inadequate, narrow notions about the nature of society and the communication process. At the risk of oversimplification, conceptualizations (if indeed such a term may be validly used here) about individuals, society and communications are media/technology-centred. Media institutions are rarely related to other institutions, or to social trends and developments within the wider social context. Moreover, the communication process tends to be shorn of its complexity and reduced to the simple cause-and-effect relationship associated with imitation and conventional attitudinal change studies.

As most of the research stems from relatively narrow, practical and commercial requirements, it tends to be fragmented, ad hoc and piecemeal. It is geared to serving 'needs' as they arise. Therefore, it is virtually incapable of contributing to the accumulation of a corpus of knowledge which is the *sine qua non* of scientific endeavour. Neither can it easily deal with the qualitative aspects of life, so again there is a tendency to reduce life and its problems and possibilities to what can be counted or measured. A further implication of this essentially atheoretical, service-oriented approach, reinforced by the fact that relevant research results from related areas tend to be ignored, is the uncritical acceptance of technological innovations as social progress. There is an undisguised, optimistic faith, which appears not to require substantiation, that there are readily available technological solutions for social problems, although it is worth noting that neither problems nor solutions are spelled out in any detail.

But all this has been said before — many times, over several years. The main justification for spelling it out once again is that one of the few unequivocal findings from communication research is that repetition is necessary. Nevertheless, having (we hope) learned from the past, we must now move forward and provide some guidelines for future research.

In general terms, in constructing these guidelines, we need to have the following considerations in mind:

1. We are dealing with a total communication process, and therefore adequate attention must be given to all those economic and political factors which govern the development of innovations, their introduction, application, output and utilization.

2. It is necessary to realize that the implications of innovations can be studied only within the appropriate historical, economic and sociological contexts, and that due attention must be given to other institutions, processes and trends.

3. Bearing in mind the implications of both the above points, particularly with regard to the appropriate contexts for introduction, application and adoption, we must explore to the full the potential of the new communication technologies for socially constructive purposes. This implies thinking in terms of *social and communication needs* and being willing to define these, rather than assume that needs (normally ill-defined) will be met by the unimpeded operation of free market forces.

4. All this implies that attention should be given to the relationship between communication policies and research policies. Enlightened communication policies depend on the information that research alone can provide. However, although information from research may be a necessary, it is never a sufficient, condition of enlightened policy — it has to be applied. It is also important to make the distinction between policy (service/administrative) research and policy-oriented research. Among other things, the latter type of research addresses policy questions without necessarily attempting to make the existing system more efficient — it attempts to relate policy to needs.

As will be seen from what follows, all these considerations are relevant at both national and international levels. In fact, in a sense, the distinction is a false one, for the two are closely interrelated. Nevertheless, Third World countries deserve special attention, particularly with regard to dependency, sovereignty and cultural identity.

Special attention must also be paid to methodological questions. This problem has already been alluded to several times, but it cannot be dealt with in full here. Let us, then, simply assert at this stage that the concepts, the techniques and the criteria of evaluation employed in conventional social science/mass communication research should no longer be allowed to determine either the questions we address or the validity of our results. We must develop a critical, eclectic methodology capable of doing justice to the complexity of our subject.

In mass communication research, as elsewhere, we can witness many different attempts by researchers from different disciplines, with different values and operating in different situations, to construct reality through their work in a variety of ways — some more systematic and soundly based than others. Given the nature of the field, and the various standpoints of the contributors, it is not surprising that the picture which emerges from all this work is less than clear. Nevertheless, while recognizing the problems which may stem from this form of pluralism, the pursuit of a range of complementary approaches is the only fruitful way of dealing with the complexities of social communications and media operations. If, in the natural sciences, it has so far been impossible to find any single theory that can explain 'everything', then surely we are not likely to find one in the social sciences. No single position or approach can be all-inclusive. Those who claim that their particular approach contains the key to all doors and the tools for all tasks clearly do not understand either the complex nature of society, its institutions and processes, or the limitations of social research.

The position advocated here is that the more complex the subject matter, the more aspects that have to be studied, then the more approaches are likely to be required to help us to formulate the many research questions which such a complex situation demands. In mass communication research we need not apologize for adopting a 'multi-perspective diagnosis'. We should seek to promote eclecticism rather than try to make excuses for it.

The plural, complementary approach from different perspectives should be adopted, primarily because it is the only one which can do justice to the complex processes and multi-faceted objects that we seek to explain and understand. Irrespective of the monopolistic positions, the over-estimations and the enthusiastic, exaggerated claims, no position is able to provide more than the partial picture of social reality permitted by its particular perspective and the limitations imposed by its conceptual framework. By its very nature, each approach leaves room for other approaches. Different phenomena, different situations and different societies may be better understood by the use of different perspectives. Moreover, this same general principle may obtain even to the same phenomena or the same society, at different times or stages of development.

Communication policies and technology

Let us now move on to a somewhat more detailed exposition of a possible research programme. Decisions are being made every day about information and communication policies and practices. In many Western industrialized countries we prefer not to think in terms of communication policies — for this smacks too much of central planning and the like. Nevertheless, policy decisions are made by many agencies, and there *is* a communication policy, albeit fragmented and latent rather than overt and consciously articulated.

When we examine policy-making in this sense with regard to information and communication, we may find that the vast majority of decisions taken with regard to communication may be classified under three headings — private profit, political expediency, and the need to maintain existing structures — and there are times when all three coincide or overlap in some way or other.

I would suggest, however, that ideally a fourth criterion should prevail, and that this should be related to *the basic information or communication needs of individuals and/or societies*. Technology should not be allowed to determine needs. Information and communication needs should be identified and evaluated from a specific value position, and then technological developments, communication policy, political and economic decisions should be formulated to meet those needs. One of the main tasks of research is to identify such needs and then to provide the information which is the prerequisite of intelligent policy formulation. This is no easy matter, but it represents an approach to information and communication problems which is much to be preferred to the approach that stems from an unholy mixture of technological and market determinism. It is certainly one that must be explored to the full, for there is ample evidence that basic communication needs will never be met by the unrestricted operation of market forces. The concept of *'public service'* is as essential in communication as it is elsewhere.

In view of 'the information explosion', one is tempted to ask, Information is the answer, but what is the question? So let us conclude by being a little more specific about the questions we should ask, and which might be addressed in research.

Who needs information? What sort of information do different groups or the population as a whole need? Why do they need it? Who decides what is needed by whom? Who selects and presents what is provided? What are the aims and intentions of the providers? What use is made of what is provided? What are the consequences of that use for individuals, groups, institutions and societies? Could what is functional for one group be dysfunctional for others, or for society as a whole? What criteria are used in determining what is functional and dysfunctional? These are just a few of the related questions that spring to mind when examining the relationship between information and communication. They are the sort of questions that should be asked by those who work in the general field of mass communication, and who study media and related institutions as social institutions, and examine communication as a social process.

Some years ago, seeking to anticipate what some people have referred to as the 'communication revolution', and in keeping with my overall research policy, I attempted to prepare a research programme to deal with these changes. I worked on the fairly obvious assumption that there was a high probability, within the next decade, that technological and organizational developments in the media, and within the communication industries generally, would be quite widespread. These developments might cover electronic publishing, video games, home computers, teletext, viewdata, video cassette recorders, video disc players, cable systems and satellites. Moreover, some countries such as the UK would experience some organizational and institutional changes — for example, obligations to serve new regions, and the development of new television channels and breakfast television. Additionally, there would be an increase in the possession of remote control sets, and in the possession of more than one set in any given household.

The application of the technology would be governed by a range of factors, including political and economic considerations, which might or might not be related to perceptions of needs. The rates of development, domestic and business, individual and societal, would differ from country to country, from innovation to innovation, and from institution to institution.

The social implications of the developments would also differ in similar fashion and would depend, among other things, on stages of development, institutional structures and arrangements, existing cultural patterns, prevailing social trends, financial resources, political decisions and so on. An appreciation of the importance of this wider, social context is vital. A basic principle of the research approach, reflecting what was suggested earlier in this paper, was that the media, new communication technologies, innovations and the communication process generally, including social implications, can only be studied adequately within the appropriate wider contexts.

The research programme, as originally formulated, had as its main general aims:

1. To examine the introduction, application and development of the new electronic and communication technologies, the factors (for instance, finance, control and organization) which influence these processes, and related institutional changes at both national and international levels.

LIBRARY ST. MARY'S COLLEGE

2. To study communication behaviour generally, and to identify and evaluate the wider social implications of the technological and institutional developments at several levels (such as attitudinal and behavioural) and in relation to other social and leisure pursuits, and other institutions such as the family and education. (The term 'social' as used here includes the economic, the political, the cultural and the religious.)

The questions and points listed below are primarily concerned with this second part, that is, with *social implications*. They may be seen as clear indications of research possibilities motivated by social concern. They are not presented here in any order of priority, and several may be asked both within a single country and between different countries.

— Will the nature and scale of the 'new communication operation' promote tendencies towards centralization and metropolitanization of information sources?
— Will people generally be more informed?
— What changes, if any, will there be in information-seeking behaviour by different groups in the population?
— Will new audiences emerge for both information and entertainment?
— Will new educational needs emerge and, if so, how will they be met?
— Will increased privatization, that is, greater concentration of home- or family-based activities, stem from the changes?
— Could the changes lead to reduced interpersonal relationships and more man–machine interaction?
— What will be the influence of the innovations on the relationship of the media to other institutions (such as church and school), and on the role of support systems and their complementary functions with regard to education, social services and social action?
— How will the new technologies be used in relation to agricultural developments, medical and health services and family planning programmes?
— Will there be an increase or decrease in the gap between the information-rich and the information-poor, and the gap between the leisure-rich and the leisure-poor? Will there be more for those who already have all the facilities, the knowledge of where to go, what to do and so forth? Will we see the further development of information/power elites?
— What about the question of dependency? Will the technologies be introduced internationally in such a way that Third World

countries become increasingly dependent on major international forces?

— Will the innovations, and the media operations generally, impede or facilitate the development of a national identity and national culture and language?

— What about the important relationship between multiplicity and diversity in both provision and use? Will more mean more of the same thing, or will there be more variety, more real choice?

— Will the changes lead to more access, more participation, more involvement, more democratization, etc. (including democratization of management and editorial functions)?

— Will the innovations lead to changes in community, and to local or regional identification at both attitudinal and behavioural levels?

— How will the new technology interact with traditional forms of communication, and what will the implications be for traditional opinion-leaders and gatekeepers?

— Will the special needs of minority and temporary membership groups be met more effectively as a result of the increase in channels?

— Will the development of consumerism be facilitated?

From a social scientific standpoint, there is a danger in producing lists of questions, problems and concerns, even when they all in some way or other address our main theme. For in adopting this list approach it is difficult to avoid both fragmentation and overlapping. There is no core, no coordinating point, no focus. What follows is a first tentative attempt to overcome this. It is by no means comprehensive, but it is hoped that it will provide what might be seen as *conceptual focal points* which, in the long run, could help us to produce a scheme more capable of being researched and more likely to lead to the establishment of a corpus of knowledge than would a long list of points and questions. Although, in one sense, it is not comprehensive in terms of the enormity of the task before us, in another sense it is too comprehensive (and too expensive) to be researched in any single exercise. Obviously, choices will have to be made and priorities established.

The essentially speculative, exploratory nature of what follows needs to be emphasized; additionally, it should be noted that the examples given under each heading are simply *examples*, and by no means exhaust what might be explored in the given area. In fact, a useful further exercise would be to go through all the above listed concerns and topics and attempt to place them within the seven categories. But, as will be seen, the categories are not mutually exclusive, and are clearly susceptible to considerable refinement and development.

Dependency. National and international, within and between countries, basically with regard to those who have and those who have not. Preservation of national culture is also relevant here.

Discrepancies. Closely related to dependency in terms of the gaps that exist, not just in relation to possessions, but also with regard to the opportunities, skills and competence that different groups have in relation to communication, and which reflect backgrounds and experiences.

Differentials. Differential pattern of use of media/new technology, reflecting, *inter alia*, some of the factors mentioned above.

Diversity. This has to do with the provision of more variety, more real choice. The meeting of the needs of minorities and other special groups, and the serving of community, local and regional interests, might all be looked at under this heading.

Displacement. The impact of the new on the old, both with regard to media and non-media institutions, including political and economic. This might also be extended to cover behavioural (time/space) changes and related institutional changes.

Democratization. New technology — media and communication systems generally, studied in relation to access, participation and involvement at all levels, including ownership, control, management and use.

Development. This concept might be extended to cover: (a) the positive, constructive or pro-social use of the media in relation to developmental goals: these could include community, education, health, social action, multi-cultural harmony and national identity, and also the other side of the coin, so to speak, namely, the present influence of the existing patterns of application in this connection; (b) development of individuals: the role of the new technology in the development of expression and creativity and in the socialization process (the links with family, school, work and so on). This subdivision could be regarded as an entirely separate category.

As mentioned earlier, present indications, such as they are, taken together with predictions based on past related experience, suggest that in many societies communication development will be governed by commercial criteria. The new media technology is likely to be introduced in such a way as to reinforce the old rather than 'create the new'.

We must also emphasize the vitally important point that, at present, the opportunities and potential for beneficial and creative use are unevenly distributed between different groups and classes within societies, as well as between different societies. Moreover, in many places the forces which sought to counter these imbalances are being eroded, and there are many signs that the gaps between rich and poor are increasing, not decreasing. Intervention is required at more than one level if we wish to go beyond reinforcing the status quo. The New International Information and Communication Order is not unrelated to the New International Economic Order.

It is essential that the ambitious claims of those who advocate the rapid adoption of new communication technologies should be seen in the light of these considerations, and put firmly to the test. Incidentally, the claims of the advocates could be used as a base for research hypotheses. Other hypotheses could be based on genuine developmental criteria.

So far, much of what has been said has been based on the assumption that the innovations will take place within existing sociopolitical-economic frameworks. At a different level, and in terms of the real potential of the new technology, it could be argued that, appropriately introduced, applied and operated (however 'appropriately' is defined), the microelectronic revolution might represent the only means at our disposal to transcend present conditions of dependency (nationally and internationally) and to combat what is often referred to as the alienation brought about by the consumer society. It could be our last opportunity to encourage creative expression and liberation.

It has been suggested that technological innovations and developments (although not on their own) could facilitate this progress by making available the information for people to act collectively, with full knowledge of the implications of their actions. They could also make possible more access, more participation, more involvement and more democratization.

Unfortunately, here again there are grounds for disquiet, for any of the above developments will depend on economic and political decisions which govern not only the innovation and application of new technologies, but also the development of the appropriate skills and competences within the general population. These will influence how and with what implications the new technologies are used. Once again, all this must be seen (at least in some parts of the world) against a background of cutbacks in the public sector, pressures towards privatization and strident cries for a return to individualism and 'Victorian values'.

We are concerned, then, with the potential of technological innovations as they impinge on the quality of life in different societies. But we need to recognize that the way in which this potential becomes activated and is eventually realized will depend on other considerations. For example, any attempts to develop the active, positive, creative, expressive, liberating use of the technology will inevitably come up not only against lack of resources, and relative deprivation, but also against past experience and the inertia of present behaviour patterns and attitudes, both of which are closely related to past and present media provision and communication behaviour. How do we transcend our experiences? How can we escape the past and make it clear that, despite commercial claims to the contrary, we are being given not what we really want (still less what we need), but what we have been conditioned to expect?

The main focus of this chapter has been on changes and developments in new technology, the media and the communication system generally. But, as always, to secure the optimum use of the media and the system, we must take into account other, non-media factors. Desired changes in the former will not be achieved without changes in the latter — it is all-round change that is required.

One final comment needs to be made, even at the risk of ending on a less than optimistic note. Research costs money, and the programme outlined here, if only partly carried out at an international comparative level, would be very expensive.

Although it is not widely accepted, there is nothing very new about the research approach and guidelines which I have just outlined. But there is a difference between advocating approaches and policies, formulating programmes and designing projects on the one hand, and being in a position and having the wherewithal to execute them on the other. In this last connection, progress has been relatively slow and modest, and the future does not appear too bright.

Although I like to think that the type of research approach favoured here represents a clear and progressive break with conventional mainstream mass communication research, I have to accept that the old beast is still alive and kicking — the old paradigm is not dead by any means. In fact, the signs are that this conventional research is more likely to be nourished and sustained in the future than the critical research which is recommended here. One doesn't have to be a clairvoyant to appreciate that those with vested interests to protect are not likely to fund research which, *inter alia*, threatens those interests by questioning basic assumptions, challenging the existing order of things and suggesting alternatives. In fact, it is more likely — and there are signs of this too — that these interests (the establishment, the elites, the powers that be) will have increasing recourse to conventional, 'scientifically valid' service research in an attempt to counter the critical thrust.

This is clearly a difficult situation, and there is no easy solution. But they are very real and pervasive practical problems which at some point have to be addressed. It is no longer possible (if it ever was before) to produce yet another inventory or list of research possibilities, without giving due attention to those economic, political, social and professional forces which obstruct or facilitate research. We would do well to recall that illuminating text from *Proverbs for Paranoids*, so indicative of mainstream mass communication research over the years: 'If they can get you to ask the wrong questions, then they don't have to worry about the answers you provide'. We shall have to fight to make sure the right questions are asked.

5

The struggle for rights and values in communication

Paul A. V. Ansah

One of the most important phenomena of the twentieth century has been the awakening and emancipation of people formerly living under colonial tutelage. The struggle for emancipation took various forms; in some countries victory was achieved after a prolonged military confrontation, while in others the colonial masters accepted the inevitable and wisely withdrew after coming to certain arrangements with their former colonies. In both cases, independence was limited to the political sphere while the economic relationship of dependence remained largely unaffected.

But regardless of the manner in which political independence or international sovereignty was achieved, the movement towards emancipation was a struggle for human dignity, the right to be heard, and the right to participate as equal partners in the sharing of the world's resources. It is this desire which led to the call for a New International Economic Order (NIEO), which was expected to establish ground rules for a more equitable distribution of the world's resources and fairer terms of trade between the industrialized nations of the North on the one hand, and the developing, raw material-producing countries of the South on the other. Most of the latter had emerged from colonial tutelage within the last thirty years.

Developments since World War II had led world leaders to the realization that, for the establishment of peace in the world, supranational bodies were needed to reconcile the conflicting interests of nations and thus reduce tension and the possibility of conflict. The development of science and technology had not only produced instruments of peace and well-being, but had also produced instruments of destruction with such potency that a genuine need was felt for international organs and principles to guide and regulate relations between states.

These international organs provided the developing countries with a platform to voice their anxieties, and they have taken full advantage of this to call for new arrangements in the political and economic spheres. The call for a New International Economic Order has thus been followed by the call for a New World Information and Communication Order (NWICO). Outside the worldwide organs, regional groupings such as the non-aligned movement have been formed to enable countries with similar problems and aspirations to speak with a collective voice in the hope that it will have greater effect.

However, in the bid to seek a more equitable redistribution of resources between the North and the South, there has been a tendency to gloss over the disparities that exist between the rich and the poor in individual countries, especially those in the South, where the gap between the 'haves' and the 'have-nots' is scandalous. In the discussion that follows, I propose to review and evaluate the collective efforts that have been made by Third World countries, with particular reference to those in Africa, to claim their rights in the sharing of the world's communication resources. This struggle for rights has been summarized in the four 'D's: Decolonization, Democratization, Demonopolization, and Development.[1]

The ultimate aim of the new structures being called for is to ensure that regional and national entities, as well as individuals, can enjoy their rights within a democratic polity in which the individual will find fulfilment. The discussion will therefore move to an evaluation of the efforts that are being made in African countries towards the democratization of communication structures and processes to ensure that individuals will be the major beneficiaries of the new orders being advocated.

The New World Information and Communication Order (NWICO)

The call for a New World Information and Communication Order arose out of the recognition by countries which had emerged from colonial domination that, in spite of political independence, the international order was controlled by the former metropolitan powers and their allies. The need to redress imbalances in the control of economic and other resources was clearly articulated by the Movement of Non-Aligned States, which at successive meetings called for both a New International Economic Order and a New International Information Order. Thanks to the efforts of UNESCO, which provided a forum for the developing countries of the Third World to air their views and grievances, the debate on the need to establish a New World Information and Communication Order (NWICO) has been made a part of the agenda for international discussion. The industrialized countries have grudgingly admitted that the developing countries have valid complaints concerning the imbalance in the distribution of information resources in the world.[2]

Some of the more familiar grievances formulated by the developing countries are related to: the imbalance in the flow of news between the North and the South; the distortions in the news about

developing countries; the preponderant influence of the transnational news agencies; and the paucity of the horizontal flow of news
among developing countries in the South, thus compelling people in
those countries to see one another from the perspective of foreign
correspondents whose value systems, ideological options and even
prejudices are often reflected in the reports. All these and other
factors culminate in a kind of media imperialism and accentuate the
dependency relationship between the developing and industrialized
countries.

These grievances are the symptoms or the results of the problem
rather than its fundamental cause, which is the wide disparity in the
sharing of resources between the affluent, industrialized countries of
the North and the impoverished, developing countries of the South.
The call for a New International Information Order (NIIO) is closely
linked with the call for a New International Economic Order
(NIEO). In fact, the two are inseparable, because it is only when
there is some equity in international economic relations that the
developing countries can afford the technical, material and human
resources needed for the development of their own communication
systems. The widening gap between the affluent and impoverished
sections of the world not only exists in terms of the volume of physical
elements, such as newspapers, magazines, books, radio, television,
telephone, telex, computer and satellite facilities; it also resides in
the fact that the developing countries are consumers of the communication products of the industrialized countries in terms of both
hardware and software, especially in the electronic media. It is this
multiple factor of technological and cultural dependence of Third
World countries based on an unjust world economic system which is
at the core of the debate on a new world order in the field of information and communication. This logically means according priority
attention to the establishment of a new economic order.

But the establishment of a New International Economic Order can
be brought about only through raising the consciousness of people
about the injustice of the existing order, and creating a worldwide
public opinion and climate that will facilitate efforts towards the
redressing of imbalances in the economic sphere. The building of this
consciousness is the responsibility of the mass media practitioners in
both the developed and the developing countries to awaken people to
the realization that, in an increasingly interdependent world,
peaceful coexistence and harmonious cooperation will be possible
only when glaring inequalities are reduced. What this means is that
the creation of a New International Economic Order and the establishment of a New World Information and Communication Order
can be legitimately seen as two phases of the same problem,

inextricably linked or mutually dependent on each other. In fact, one scholar sees NWICO as a sub-system of a NIEO rather than as a complement to it.[3]

The relentless efforts made by the developing countries to have issues of a new world order of communication included in the agenda for international discussion stemmed from their recognition that, although the development of telecommunication facilities had opened up immense possibilities for the flow of information among individuals, nations and regions, the question of how developing countries could derive maximum benefit for their social advancement and cultural development remained to be settled. The aim of NWICO was thus meant to set in motion 'a process of building up a worldwide international information and communications systems, which will permit multi-directional, multi-dimensional, equitable international communications in the interest of all nations and of all peoples of the world'.[4]

The concern of the developing countries was to ensure that the vast potential offered by innovations in communication technology could be harnessed to promote cultural progress, social development and international understanding rather than to perpetuate the subjugation to which they had been relegated by historical circumstances. They also wanted to ensure that they could take advantage of the world's communication resources to articulate their problems and make their own contribution to world culture, rather than remaining passive recipients of other people's cultures which could undermine their cultural integrity and identities.

Another factor which spurred the Third World countries on to call for a new international information order was the realization that, for new nations which had endured various degrees of cultural assimilation from their colonial masters, and which needed a kind of cultural renaissance as a foundation for self-reliant development, an unregulated and unreciprocated flow of mass media offerings from the developed countries through direct satellite broadcasts and similar devices could weaken the fabric of society and undermine its indigenous social, cultural and political values, thereby rendering the task of nation-building more difficult. One objective of NWICO, therefore, is to encourage a consensus that will ensure that international understanding can be promoted through freely established cultural contacts and a fair and balanced flow of information, rather than through an unbalanced, one-way flow which may eventually result in what has been called 'cultural imperialism' or 'cultural synchronization'.[5]

The efforts of the developing nations of the Third World to press for the creation of NWICO have not been limited to debates in international forums; they have been backed up by concrete acts which, though perhaps not spectacular, nevertheless constitute a practical demonstration of their resolve and ambitions or aspirations. In this context, it is worth citing the establishment of regional and interregional organizations such as the News Agencies Pool of the Non-Aligned Countries, Inter-Press Service (IPS), the Caribbean News Agency (CANA), the Asia Pacific Broadcasting Union, the Organization of Asian News Agencies (OANA), the Asia–Pacific News Network (ANN), the Pan-African News Agency (PANA) and the Union of African National Radio and Television (URTNA), among others.[6]

The setting up of such regional bodies is based on the belief by the participating countries that collective efforts on their part in the supply of news, the training of journalists and the exchange of technology and programmes within the constraints of their limited resources will enable them to speed up the process of reducing their dependence on the industrialized countries of the North. The initial expectations have not been fulfilled, however, and the situation has been aggravated by the increasingly difficult economic situation worldwide in which the poorer countries are worse off; but the laying of the necessary foundations already constitutes some progress on the march towards redressing the imbalance and promoting a horizontal flow of communication.

The communication explosion and the Third World
The technology that sustains communication is developing at such a rapid pace that one can legitimately speak of a communication explosion. Information gathering, processing, storage and retrieval systems are being developed so fast that the world seems to be overfed with information. But while there seems to be a glut of information in certain parts of the world, there is a dearth of information in others.

This is because information and communication technology is capital-intensive and requires huge financial outlays which the overburdened and overheated economies of the developing countries cannot afford. This means that large amounts of information can be gathered about the developing countries and used for all sorts of purposes, without their being able to get access to it or to send out information about themselves. The Third World countries are thus becoming increasingly dependent on the advanced countries for their information needs, and the gap is widening rather than narrowing. This widening gap further underscores the direct relationship between the New International Economic Order (NIEO) and the New World Information and Communication Order (NWICO).

The communication explosion thus hardly constitutes a concrete reality to most Third World countries because they cannot take full advantage of the range of possibilities offered owing to lack of resources. They have to depend on the goodwill of the industrialized nations, which control both the technology and the resources needed to purchase it. At the level of the developing countries, the lack of appropriate infrastructure constitutes the main obstacle to taking advantage of innovations in the field of telecommunications. Africa is the poorest region of the world in terms of telephones. Those few receivers available are concentrated in the urban areas, and even there are limited to a super-elite. The more sophisticated the gadgets become, the more restricted is the number of those who can get access to them, as in the case of the cordless telephone. But the point needs to be made that, with better management and political goodwill, it should still be possible to organize things so that even the rudimentary telecommunications facilities are more equitably redistributed.

The paradox of the situation is that, for the developing countries of Africa, 'more' in fact means 'less' within the context of the information explosion. The developments in information technology have created a situation in which those who control wealth or political power will have access to increasing volumes of information, which they can manipulate for their own ends at the expense of the majority of underprivileged people who will have very little information. This is valid at both the national and the international level. The wealthy countries of the North will have more information readily at their disposal, while the poorer nations of the South can get access to very little.

At the level of individual countries, those in the urban areas at the centre will have access to more information, and can thereby strengthen their dominant position, because they have the infrastructure and the means to purchase both equipment and programmes, while those on the periphery in the rural areas will see even their little power diminished because they lack both the most rudimentary infrastructure and the means to purchase receiving equipment and programmes. In the developing countries, the kind of information to which the 'haves' will have access will be almost the same as what the wealthy in the industrialized countries will receive, so that the wealthy minorities in the poorer countries will become alienated from the cultural values and social concerns of the poorer sections of their community. One can therefore endorse the apt observation that 'the "information revolution" will have no geographical boundaries. It will not stop at the equator. Its boundaries, however, will be social. In the Third World it will concentrate on the big cities and on those with money.'7

To solve the problem of this widening gap, which is being aggravated by advances in technological innovations, what is needed is a basic reordering of priorities and serious efforts at social restructuring. Economic opportunities and prospects for social mobility in developing countries are so limited, and so unevenly distributed between the centre and the periphery, that even the extension of infrastructures such as electrification and telecommunication lines to the rural areas will constitute a token gesture, because the people do not command sufficient financial resources to be able to afford receiving sets or maintenance costs. The provision of basic social amenities to the majority of the people living in rural areas in Africa hardly engages the serious attention of policy-makers, despite the populist rhetoric and the pious declarations of concern for the welfare of the underprivileged.

The major problem facing the development of information technology in Africa is that policy-makers appear to have got their priorities wrong. Instead of continuing efforts to provide basic infrastructures and extending them through the whole of society, attention seems to be focused on more sophisticated technology which benefits only a small section of the national community. This only reflects the situation in which power is held by a minority who make little or no effort to bring the people closer to the decision-making processes within that society.

Of course, it is not being suggested that developing countries should try to run their affairs without resorting to the possibilities offered by the new information technology; in fact, even if they wanted to, they could not. Computer facilities and information transmitted by satellite are necessary for the building of data bases which will make national planning more meaningful. Information on long-range weather forecasts, research in agriculture, the monitoring of market trends and the compilation of accurate and up-to-date national statistics are all made possible through the use of the new information technology. If this technology were to be used mainly for such developmental purposes, the benefits would accrue to the whole population, and it would be wise use of national resources. Unfortunately, the evidence in both the advanced and the developing countries suggests that, particularly with respect to the 'video revolution', there is much more concentration on entertainment than on development issues, and this reduces the usefulness of the technological innovations and limits the number of potential beneficiaries.

Those who are developing the new information technology are aware that they cannot maximize profits and reach the widest market if their products are to be limited to official, business and industrial users. The way to widen the market is to link up with the entertainment industries to provide the appropriate software that will appeal to larger groups of people, including the privileged classes in the developing countries. This is the point that Allen Greenberg makes when he writes: 'Third World telecommunications are — or at least should be — of considerable interest to the United States, for reasons ranging from enlightened altruism to the bread-and-butter concerns of trade balances and jobs'.[8]

Communication realities in Africa

As has been stated earlier, one major characteristic of communication systems in Africa is the very glaring disparity between urban and rural areas in terms of the distribution of media resources, as well as other services. Following the colonial pattern, the physical development of good housing, clean drinking water, motorable roads and hospitals has been concentrated in cities and large towns. In the same way, media facilities are concentrated in the urban areas. Newspapers are produced in the cities and distributed mainly in the urban areas where most of the literates live. Television is not available in the rural areas where the vast majority of the people live because such areas lack the requisite infrastructure; besides, television sets are priced out of the reach of most rural dwellers.

Radio can be considered a truly mass medium in Africa because the transistor revolution has reached the rural dwellers, though in some countries the centralized radio systems are unable to cater for the needs of small linguistic groups. In terms of content, however, much of the information contained in newspapers is of little or no relevance to the concerns of the rural people, and most of the television fare is alien even to large sections of the urban dwellers. Evidence abounds to demonstrate that media facilities are very underdeveloped in Africa.

Apart from radio, then, it is newspapers and television that deal mainly with issues of interest to the urban minority. As one study found out, 'it is becoming increasingly clear that our newspapers are being used by the well-connected in underwriting the privileged status of urban social classes — politicians, and administrative, military and professional elites. This is probably to be expected as mass media facilities are to be found mainly in urban areas in Ghana'.[9] This observation holds true for most African countries.

Even though the newspaper can therefore be properly considered a minority medium, its contents and influence are spread much wider than the small circulation figures would suggest. The use of the newspaper to mobilize the people in the struggle against colonialism proves this claim. The written word provided the material to feed the interpersonal channels of communication. In this connection it is worth recalling the words of Kwame Nkrumah, who made very effective use of the newspaper medium in his political campaigns: 'The reach of the press is, of course, narrower in areas where there is a high degree of illiteracy; but even in those areas the people can always be reached by the spoken word. And frequently the written word becomes the spoken word'.[10]

Many reasons can be found to explain the slow and lopsided development of media facilities in Africa. The first is economic: because of a difficult economic situation, the physical infrastructure to sustain a modern mass media system is lacking. For the same reason, the great pressure on limited foreign exchange does not permit the allocation of adequate resources to the importation of newsprint, equipment or other consumables and spares for running the system. This is something that African countries can do little about as long as their economies stagnate or regress.

But a more important reason for the slow growth of communication facilities and their uneven distribution is poor management. It is contended here that, even within the limits of the meagre resources available, more careful planning and sensible management would enable existing facilities to be more equitably distributed throughout the country. For example, many African countries operate external broadcasting services for the purpose of projecting their national personality and as an instrument of foreign policy. In many cases this is just another symbol of independence. These external services have very good transmission and studio facilities, which would be more profitably employed to augment the inadequate national service.

In addition, the officials managing the publicly owned media systems in Africa appear to be fascinated by gadgetry, and they go in for sophisticated press and radio equipment where simpler versions would be quite adequate. The result is that they become bound to change their equipment as more advanced versions become available on the market, thus using up more of their scarce resources.

It must, of course, be conceded that in certain cases it is not really a question of choice. The situation of colour television will be used to illustrate the point. In almost all African countries, television is an elite medium which serves a tiny minority of urban dwellers. Because of the advances in technology, however, the monochrome set is becoming an endangered species, and it is increasingly difficult to obtain spares to service the existing ones. For this reason, even those countries which consider that efforts in terms of priorities should be geared towards extending television signals to other parts of the country are compelled to go into colour; and in view of the cost of receiving sets, it is obvious that still fewer people in the urban areas can afford to purchase them, thus restricting the distribution of television services even more.

The paradox is that, while the new technology is giving people in industrialized countries greater access to communication facilities, in the developing countries it is making the facilities available to smaller numbers and thus widening the gap between the various sections of the national communities.

Whatever the external constraints, it can be forcefully argued that a better appreciation of the need to establish effective national communication systems, which will provide channels for dialogue between the leaders and the people and furnish information for intelligent participation in decision-making, will lead to a more rational use of limited resources. A considerable portion of the investments made, particularly in the areas of television and external broadcasting, cannot be subjected to rational cost–benefit analysis.

But the reasons for the uneven and slow development of the mass media in Africa go beyond the scarcity of resources, lack of infrastructure and poor management of the mass media. Even the regular flow of information through interpersonal channels is subject to political intolerance. Since the mass media system of a country is a reflection of its political, social, economic and cultural structures, it is unrealistic to expect a democratic communication system in authoritarian or totalitarian regimes of either the civilian or the military variety. In such regimes, political and economic power as well as social privileges are monopolized by minorities who see the free flow of information and the freedom of expression as a threat to their power. A new information order is therefore needed at the national level in the name of social and political justice. The kind of rights being claimed by the Third World countries at the international level must be seen to operate at the various national levels in the developing countries.

Mass media and development in Africa

No account of the nationalist struggle in Africa, at least in the former British colonies, would be complete without reference to the role played by the press in awakening nationalist consciousness. The nationalist leaders, taking advantage of the relatively liberal atmosphere of the period, even by colonial standards, established newspapers for mobilizing the people.[11]

Soon after independence, however, the new national leaders, having learnt from personal experience the power that the press could wield in mobilizing people against oppressive regimes, set about systematically dismantling the press models they had inherited, and establishing in their place their own authoritarian models. Opposition or privately owned newspapers were forced out of existence through the application of legal, political, economic and other pressures. Relations between governments and an independent press have thus, since independence, been characterized by conflict and tension, constitutional guarantees of freedom of the press notwithstanding.

Another characteristic of the media systems in Africa is the dominant or monopolistic situation enjoyed by the government in the ownership, control and operation of both the print and electronic media. The justification given for this state of affairs is that, in order to use the mass media for the promotion of national integration and the achievement of national development objectives, it is essential that the media be guided and directed by the government.

A further reason given for the close involvement of the government with media operations in Africa is that the government needs channels through which it can explain its plans and policies to the people and ensure that they are adequately, regularly and accurately informed and educated about national objectives. The government's own organs, the argument continues, are more likely to discharge these functions than private entrepreneurs, whose selection processes and perceptions may be at variance with those of the government.

The case for African governments operating newspapers and other publications was clearly articulated by a Ghanaian parliamentarian when he said:

> The press in a developing country is a vital organ of Government and, whether we like it or not, it has a greater potential for good or ill than it has in a more developed country. In Britain or America, for example, opinions are expressed in dozens of privately owned newspapers. Any view can be challenged, analysed and looked at from every direction, and the average reader is given the opportunity of making up his mind. This situation is not so in a developing country, and so it is important that opinion that gets to the people is as unbiased as possible. . . . The Government has a duty to the people, and it is important that its views are clearly reported and not twisted in any way. For that reason, there is a case for the Government having a press where its views will not be distorted.[12]

In developing countries, beyond their traditional functions, the mass media are assigned the additional role of acting as support for development, and this has given rise to the 'developmental theory' of the press. This theory, which has been articulated by Hachten and McQuail, among other communication scholars, has been functionally described as 'developmental communication', 'development communication' and 'development support communication'. The concept was first systematically developed by Asian communication scholars at the University of the Philippines at Los Baños (UPLB), but the invention of the concept of communication as a support for development is attributed to Erskine Childers.

It is not easy to give a precise and neat definition of the concept, especially as it is assumed to be applicable to a number of developing countries at various stages of development and with a great variety of economic and political systems as well as cultural norms and social structures. However, from the emerging body of literature on the subject, one can isolate the following elements: the media should carry out positive development tasks as defined by the national policy-makers; the state has the right to restrict media operations and exercise direct control; the operational model should not be from the centre to the periphery; special efforts should be made in the promotion of national culture and integration; greater emphasis should be put on collective ends rather than on individual rights and freedoms.

The concept of 'development communication' is yet to be clearly defined and its interpretation is still under debate. In 1971, Nora C. Quebral defined it as 'the art and science of human communication applied to the speedy transformation of a country and the mass of its people from poverty to a dynamic state of economic growth that makes possible greater social equality and the longer fulfilment of the human potential'.[13] Originally, the concept was applied in a limited way to the use of communication techniques in relation to agriculture, health, family planning and so on, but in the course of time it has been broadened to mean generally 'communication with a social conscience'.[14]

In many developing countries, particularly those in Africa, the need for rapid national development has given rise to the establishment of authoritarian and monolithic political institutions in which basic human rights and freedoms have been suppressed. The question then is, Are authoritarian controls necessary or even desirable for development communication? There are at least two schools of thought on this issue. Writing on the influence of the authoritarian press on the elaboration of the 'developmental theory' of the press, Mort Rosenblum tries to articulate, or at least to rationalize, the position of Third World leaders in these words:

> The basic approach is that all national resources, including the resource of information, must be directed toward development. If information is allowed to cause dissent or loss of international prestige, it detracts from the greater goal. By this reasoning, the control of news is not only a legitimate right, but also a national necessity.[15]

This interpretation of development communication or development journalism puts the press in an abjectly subservient position to the government and reduces it to a mere mouthpiece or megaphone for the government. There is, however, another interpretation of the concept, which assigns to the media a watchdog role, consisting of scrutinizing the activities of the government in the area of development by measuring performance against promise. This second school of thought sees the relation between the developmental journalist and the government as one of a critical observer rather than an obsequious and uncritical advocate. This point is succinctly made by Narinder Aggarwala, when he writes that the responsibility of the communicator involved in development journalism is to:

> Critically examine, evaluate and report the relevance of a development project to national and local needs, the difference between a planned scheme and its actual implementation, and the differences between its impact on people as claimed by government officials and as it actually is.[16]

This is an enlightened view of development communication, which shows that communication need not make a positive contribution to national development only in an atmosphere of stringent authoritarian controls. While conceding that the purposeful use of communication for development calls for a certain measure of direction, the problem really lies in how to define the modalities for providing the media with direction. A certain amount of cooperation with the government is needed in order to get to know its development thinking and priorities, if for no other reason than that the government is an important catalyst in the development process, and thus an important source of information on development issues.

But such cooperation need not, and should not, degenerate into the type of sycophancy and subservience that precludes a critical appraisal of the government's development priorities, promises and actual performance. In other words, the need for rapid development should not be allowed to constitute for the government a pretext for exercising authoritarian control over the media; nor should it lead media personnel to abdicate their social responsibility to act as watchdogs of the people's interests.

Perhaps it is pertinent to point out that the thinking which sees the rights of self-expression and development as being in antithetical position to each other is based on a mechanistic and erroneous concept of development. 'Development' has been defined as 'a widely participatory process of social change in a society, intended to bring about both social and material advancement (including greater equality, freedom and other valued qualities) for the majority of the people through their gaining greater control over their environment'.[17]

Given this concept of development, the question that arises is, How do people gain control over their environment when they are not free or have no opportunity or channels to express their views about their environment in its various aspects — social, political, economic or cultural? Popular participation is considered an essential ingredient in this new concept of development, and for total human development the involvement of the populace is necessary; such involvement can be secured only if people have a say in the planning and execution of programmes for development.

This means that, for development to occur, there should be not only a review of social structures, but also a reorganization of the communication delivery system to ensure that it moves from the one-way, top–bottom, vertical direction to incorporate at least a regular feedback system that is two-way, bottom–up and horizontal. If popular participation is a prerequisite for effective and integral human development, it is clear that the provision of facilities and opportunities for free self-expression through the media or interpersonal channels is an aid to development rather than a hindrance to it, contrary to the myths that have been purveyed by many Third World leaders for self-serving purposes.

Information flow and the democratic process

The process of communication is so basic to social interaction, to the articulation of social aspirations and to the maintenance of community or national values that its smooth operation becomes a useful index for determining the political equilibrium within a society. It is essential not only because it helps in the socialization of the individual, but also because it helps to direct the society towards integral human development.

Information, which is the raw material of communication, should thus be treated as a social good rather than a marketable commodity regulated by economic forces alone. Since people need information to be able to live responsibly in society, it should be made available in the same way that other basic social needs are provided. It is this realization that has led to the consideration of the right to communicate as a fundamental human right, enabling people to inform themselves, form judgements, evaluate the performance of their rulers, and protect their individual and collective social interests.

Another concept which has come into prominence in the course of the NWICO debate is the 'right to communicate'. Not unexpectedly, the campaign for the recognition of this right has provoked a lot of controversy. There are those who argue that this right can be properly assumed under Article 19 of the Universal Declaration of Human Rights, which guarantees freedom of opinion and expression as well as the right to seek, receive and impart information through any media. There are others who argue that technological changes have altered the situation and added new dimensions to such an extent that a specific 'right to communicate' is called for. The debate has been going on since the 18th General Conference of UNESCO in 1984. The main point of contention seems to be the locus of this right — whether it should belong to individuals, to groups, or to whole nations. Because of the different political and philosophical positions with regard to the relationship between the individual and society, it will be some time before the concept is given a widely acceptable definition within the framework of NWICO.[18]

However the concept of the 'right to communicate' is eventually defined, its main objective is to ensure that facilities are made available to individuals and various social groups for the interchange of information on a more equal footing. In other words, it not only calls for more abundant information from a plurality and diversity of sources, but it also seeks to provide opportunities to reciprocate, so that there is a balanced, two-way flow between the various participants in the communication process. In sum, its purpose is to democratize communication.

In many developing countries, even where the mass media have a limited reach, they constitute an important source of information and education to the majority of the people on national issues. They thus function as an important instrument for the permanent education of the countries' inhabitants. Given this important role of the mass media, it can be considered one of the major elements in the achievement of democracy. In Africa, the general pattern of media ownership is one of government or party control, with a number of privately owned newspapers or magazines existing side by side in the few countries where political pluralism is tolerated.

The specific place of the mass media in the democratic process is open to question in Africa. They are generally controlled by the ruling elite, who use them to manipulate the people rather than as channels for rational discourse on national issues. The state-owned media tend to exclude the views of those who are not in agreement with the government. The private press is usually so feeble, and subject to such pressures by the government, that often it cannot provide a genuinely alternative source of information or channel for the exchange of views. It follows from this that the basic ownership and control structures do not adequately reflect the various classes, perceptions, interest groups and political preferences in the society.

Where pluralism is found, it is only what Juan Somavia calls 'formal pluralism', reflecting 'a vision of the world as seen by an affluent and powerful minority of society', controlling either political or economic power or both.[19]

The issue of the democratization of mass communication revolves around the concepts of access to media facilities and participation in media policy formulation and programming. In the industrialized countries, the question of access has been handled through a highly decentralized system as seen in community media, which ensure a relatively greater say in programming. But such an arrangement is possible only in certain socio-cultural contexts which are not found in the African situation. Despite the possible advantages to be derived from a decentralized media system, the political realities of many Third World countries do not favour its adoption. As Amunugama rightly observes:

> Unlike the developed nations, which have a coherent political and cultural polity, the product of many years' evolution, most Third World countries have not yet consolidated a national identity. The transition from regional, tribal, ethnic, religious or caste loyalty to national identity has not been completed.[20]

For this reason it is felt that, whereas the resources of a centralized national media system can be harnessed for the creation of a feeling of national cohesion and integration, a decentralized system will render the task of creating national symbols and a national identity more difficult. Far from ensuring that the voices of various interest and social groups are heard, a decentralized system may result in fragmentation and divisiveness.[21]

The new technology has made it possible for local communities in the industrialized countries to get involved with communications as both producers and consumers. This has been achieved within the framework of community communications, which enables people to develop their own communication services, including press, video, radio, film, television and other resources. The body responsible for community communications also undertakes campaigns to seek funding for its services from private and public sources. Such groups have been campaigning for the promise that broadcasting policies will be revised to establish a statutory right to local community ownership and operation of radio and television stations. The ultimate objective is to obtain effective participation in local, regional and national communication and information policies, so that control can become more democratic.

Contrary to the situation in the industrialized countries, the question of democratizing communication in Africa has not become a topical issue. Despite the recognition that people need information to enable them to participate actively in social and political life, the production, processing and dissemination of information is limited to a small professional elite or to those who wield economic or political power. The poorer sections of the community are thus excluded from contributing effectively to the formation of national culture. For this reason, the structure of modern communication in Africa is vertical, with the one-way flow going from top to bottom, 'where the few talk to the many about the needs and problems of the many from the standpoint of the few'.[22]

The question of what is to be done to ensure that communication is effectively democratized in Africa is a thorny one. In addition to the lack of infrastructure and political intolerance mentioned earlier, the high level of illiteracy constitutes a major obstacle. In order to participate effectively in the operating or management of the mass media, a certain level of literacy is a prerequisite. With an average literacy level of about 30 percent in most of black Africa, even if the structures were established, it would be difficult for the people to take full advantage of the situation, to become not only receivers but also originators of media content or at least of media policy.

Gerhard Maletzke proposes three ways of democratizing communication, namely, Inter-action, Co-production and Co-determination, and he sees Co-determination as the closest to the democratizing process. He writes: 'The underlying concept of Co-determination is that the citizens should co-determine what should go on in mass communication, that they should co-determine the general policy as well as the programming of the media.'[23] This means that the determination of message content should not be limited to an elite minority of professionals or power brokers, but should be decided by a broadly based group representing various social, political and economic interests.

Co-determination thus calls for a change in media structures to reflect the various shades of opinion and interest groups within the society. Realistically, all that can be expected is that, at the policy-making level, there should be a democratic representation of views to reflect the diversity and pluralism of society. The idea is not to take over the professional functions of media personnel, but to enrich the communication process 'by broadening the communicators' criteria, values and processing methods'.

It is towards the achievement of this object that highly localized and 'alternative' media systems have been established in several parts of the world. For a number of reasons, however, one forecast is that it will take a very long time before African countries move in this particular direction. Widespread illiteracy, the absence of appropriate infrastructure and, most importantly, political considerations make this type of development rather premature. Nevertheless, the traditional communication structures can be so strengthened that at the village, district or regional level people will become not only receivers of information but also sources of information.

A reordering of priorities
The debate on NWICO has had one positive effect in Africa by focusing attention on communication problems and getting the leaders to give some thought to the role of communication in society. However, reflections on communication issues have not always been accompanied by the necessary open-mindedness. The result is that, where further resources are committed, these are not always channelled into the areas where they are most needed, namely, the deprived sections of the community. Besides, fascination with gadgetry seems to take precedence over functional effectiveness, with the result that there is a tendency to catch up with the advanced countries in terms of equipment sophistication.

On the fundamental issues involved in NWICO, developments in some African countries have been less than satisfactory. The whole debate is about the democratization of communication — how to get all sections of the community to participate in democratic dialogue through a regular and free flow of communication. In addition to the physical, technical and economic constraints referred to, the major obstacle to the democratization of communication appears to be the political intolerance that one sees in most African countries. And to the extent that the mass media system is a reflection of the social, political, economic and cultural environment in which it operates, no meaningful moves towards democratic communication institutions can be made without a fundamental restructuring of the social and political order.

Since information constitutes an important base for political and economic power, the powerful in society, who do not want to see their power eroded, will do everything they can to limit the flow of information. In the African situation, far from advances in communication technology bringing about a wider distribution of information, distribution is paradoxically restricted to those who already have more than their fair share of information. The incidence of widespread illiteracy also constitutes a major hurdle to be cleared before we move closer towards democratic communication institutions.

Because of various forms of restriction, people at the grassroots level have not asserted their rights as citizens in a democratic polity. Where they have been mobilized to fight for their rights, experience has shown them that those who lead them in the struggle do not take long to divest them of their democratic gains. These new leaders claim to speak in the name of the people, who are denied the opportunity to articulate their own views through either the modern mass media or the traditional communication channels.

At times, the need for accelerated national development has been used as a pretext to close all avenues for democratic dialogue. I have tried to show that this approach betrays a fundamental misconception of development because people have the right to ask questions such as, What kind of development? Development for whom? Development at what rate and at what cost? The evidence in Africa certainly shows that the most authoritarian regimes are by no means the most developed in material or human terms.

The reordering of priorities in Africa is basic to any move towards a new order of economics or information. Even if it were possible to arrive at arrangements which could ensure a more equitable redistribution of the world's resources and establish a fairer system of international trade, the resources that will become available may only go to augment the privileges of the 'haves' at the expense of the welfare of the 'have-nots' as long as the present social structures remain.

Technology can only provide additional tools; what is made of the new tools depends on those who put them to use. The issue, then, is basically the human material that one has to work with, and the available evidence suggests that this is one of the resources of which Africa stands in the greatest need. This is why the 'communication revolution' will not become a concrete reality for many Third World countries for a long time to come.

Notes

1. Kaarle Nordenstreng, 'Defining the New International Information Order', p. 34 in George Gerbner and Marsha Siefert (eds), *World Communication — A Handbook*. New York: Longman, 1983.

2. The most comprehensive accounts of the NWICO debate can be found in (a) UNESCO, *Many Voices — One World*, Report by the International Commission for the Study of Communication Problems (popularly known as the 'MacBride Report'). London: Kogan Page; New York: Unipub; Paris: UNESCO, 1980. (b) K. Nordenstreng and L. Hannikainen, *The Mass Media Declaration of UNESCO*. Norwood, NJ: Ablex Publishing, 1984. This is a historical account of the NWICO debate at UNESCO. It also deals with issues of international law and professional ethics and includes 27 appendices containing the declarations and documents from various drafting stages.

3. Jan Pronk, 'Some Remarks on the Relation between the New International Information Order and the New International Economic Order', 1978. Document 35 of the MacBride Commission. On the relations between the two orders, see also Cees J.

Hamelink, *Cultural Autonomy in Global Communications*. New York: Longman, 1983.

4. Bogdan Osolnik, 'Aims and Approaches to a New International Communication Order', 1978. Document 32 of the MacBride Commission.

5. Hamelink, op. cit., p. 5. Hamelink explains his preference for the term 'cultural synchronisation' as follows: 'In the international literature, this phenomenon is usually described as cultural imperialism. I give preference to the concept of cultural synchronisation, which is more precise for my purposes. In my view, cultural imperialism is the most frequent, but not exclusive, form in which cultural synchronisation occurs. Cultural synchronisation can take place without imperialistic relations constituting the prime causal factor or even without any overt imperialistic relations.'

6. For a detailed description of such regional effects, see Hamelink, op. cit., pp. 72–8.

7. 'Information Technology and the Third World', *Media Development*, 30(4):1.

8. Allen Greenberg, 'Impasse: The US Stake in Third World Telecommunications Development', *Journal of Communication*, 1985, 35(2):42.

9. Yaw Twumasi, 'Social Class and Newspaper Coverage in Ghana', p. 211 in Frank O. Ugboajah (ed.), *Mass Communication, Culture and Society in West Africa*. Oxford: Hans Zell Publishers, 1985.

10. Kwame Nkrumah, *Africa Must Unite*. London: Panaf Books, 1963.

11. One could cite publications such as Kwame Nkrumah's *Evening News*, Nnamdi Azikiwe's *West African Pilot*, Jomo Kenyatta's *Mwigwithania* and Herbert Macauley's *Lagos Daily News*, among others. For further details see Rosalynde Ainslie, *The Press in Africa*, London: Gollancz, 1966; William A. Hachten, *Muffled Drums*, Ames: Iowa State University Press, 1971; Graham Mytton, *Mass Communication in Africa*, London: Edward Arnold, 1983.

12. Debate on the Newspaper Licensing (Repeal) Bill, *Ghana Parliamentary Debates* (1970), 2(297).

13. Nora C. Quebral, 'What Do We Mean by Development Communication?' *International Development Review*, 1973, 15(2):2.

14. Nora C. Quebral, 'Development Communication: Where Does It Stand Today?' *Media Asia*, 1975, 2(4):198.

15. Mort Rosenblum, *Coups and Earthquakes*. New York: Harper & Row, 1979.

16. Narinder Aggarwala, 'What is Development News?' *Journal of Communication* 1979, 29(2):181.

17. Everett M. Rogers, 'Communication and Development: The Passing of the Dominant Paradigm', *Communication Research*, 1976, 3(2):225.

18. Desmond Fisher, 'The Achievement of a New Right to Communicate', *Intermedia*, 1983, 11(3):36–40.

19. Juan Somavia, 'The Democratization of Communications', *Development Dialogue*, 1981(2):19.

20. Sarath Amunugama, 'Communication Issues Confronting the Developing Nations', p. 59 in George Gerbner and Marsha Siefert (eds), *World Communications — A Handbook*. New York: Longman, 1983.

21. For a fuller discussion, using Ghana as an example, see Paul A.V. Ansah, 'Problems of Localising Radio in Ghana', *Gazette*, 1979, 25(4):1–16.

22. UNESCO, *Many Voices — One World*, op. cit.

23. George Maletzke, 'Participation in Mass Communication', *Media Asia*, 1975, 2(3):167.

6

Leapfrogging the industrial revolution

Usha V. Reddi

Walking in space. Capturing an errant satellite and repairing it. Communicating instantaneously with any part of the world. Shopping without stepping out of the home. Enjoying fewer hours of work, more hours of leisure. All these were fantastic visions in the nineteenth century. One hundred years later, on the threshold of the twenty-first century, these visions are a reality, a part of daily life, for those fortunate enough to enjoy them. But for the majority of the world's population, such achievements are still a distant dream.

To bring the fruits of technological development without further delay to the underdeveloped regions of the world, while ensuring an equitable distribution of wealth, is the objective of development planners throughout the world. Is there hope that the new revolution will enable humans to eradicate poverty with its concomitant social and psychological aspects? A quantum leap is required, a leap from the traditional stages of progress to the most sophisticated technological society, and in such a short time as to catch up with the industrial and developed nations of the world.

Little need be said of conditions in the developing countries. Widespread poverty, illiteracy, disease and economic despair are the order of the day. Added to this is the exploitation which has resulted in an unending cycle of underdevelopment. But far more important, political awareness has preceded economic development, resulting in social conflicts and the demand for a better life immediately. For the developing countries, using modern technology is like using the lift instead of the staircase, moving rapidly to the most modern methods while bypassing all the transitional stages.

Social change and national development for countries that have made the historical transition from agrarian to industrial societies have resulted from three fundamental social revolutions: economic, political, and communication. All three were spread over a period of three centuries at a time when colonialism was the norm rather than the exception. The economic revolution entailed the transformation of a society from subsistence and self-sufficiency to commodity production.[1] This process of industrialization was aided in large measure by the successful exploitation of the natural resources of weaker nations, where the prices of raw materials were kept abnor-

84

mally low, and where it was possible for the stronger nations to conquer militarily and dominate politically.

The second revolution, which followed quickly on the heels of economic transformation, was political, involving the rise of political consciousness and nationalism, the transition from forms of political subjugation to patterns of participatory government. The political mobilization of the masses which took place after the economic revolution in the developed countries was influenced by the writings of Locke and Rousseau.[2]

The communication revolution of the twentieth century has gone beyond the expectations of most people by inducing far-reaching and irreversible changes in life-styles. It has made possible a transition from oral societies to multi-media interactive systems; it has cut continental distances into mere 'hop-overs'; it has rendered old concepts of national sovereignty and boundaries meaningless; it has generated a new educational technology that makes learning available to everyone, regardless of location and distance. The communication revolution has fostered rising expectations and frustrations and the growth of mass cultures, and has enabled social and political mobilization and integration to occur. In the developed countries, the communication revolution has heralded the information society.

For the developing countries, this multi-dimensional process (economic, political and communications) has created historic challenges and opportunities as well as problems and contradictions of monumental proportions. But of one thing we can be sure: in these countries, the political and communication revolutions have preceded economic transformation. Economic development has not kept pace with political consciousness, and the communication technologies available have altered the very assumptions and concepts underlying planning.

The problems of growth and development in the former colonies have many dimensions, and infrastructures are needed to provide an opportunity for all individuals to realize their fullest potential. These systems must grow within the context of the diverse and contradictory compulsions and needs of the society, including geographical inequalities, cultural diversities, scarcities of manpower and finance, and political requirements of cohesion, mobilization and legitimacy.

The entire development process which encompassed three centuries in the industrial nations must be telescoped into a few decades. The gains achieved through an evolutionary process elsewhere must be obtained within one generation, and there are several strategies to planning. Some nations have arrived at their individual strategies by default or as a consequence of economic or political considerations. Others have chosen policies suited to their specific conditions. One of these strategies is to leapfrog the industrial revolution, proceeding to the most sophisticated technological advances and using these to spearhead the development process, rather than supporting it by pushing from behind.

In today's world, it is the technologically superior countries which command the destinies of their own and other nations, be it in economic, political, military or other spheres. All countries are scrambling to acquire the most advanced technological systems, sometimes without giving serious thought to the consequences of that technology.

Much has been said about the current technological revolution, particularly in the field of communications, and its present and potential impact upon society. The central factor in this revolution is, of course, the space satellite, with multi-point connections, enormous circuit capacity and low cost per circuit (compared with conventional and terrestrial systems), in terms of both quality and reliability. On earth, the computer with the microchip has opened up new avenues for the speedy, reliable and cost-effective transmission of information. The computer has enabled people to do away with much of the tedium in information storage, processing and retrieval. Computer-assisted instruction has caused a revolution in teaching methodology, made possible electronic word processing and electronic mail, and taken the humdrum out of much work, so that people can expand the frontiers of their knowledge, broaden the horizon of their outlook and adopt a more meaningful way of life.

The technical feasibility to do this rests on several factors: (1) knowledge and capacity for handling space hardware and technology; (2) improvement of performance and reliability through advanced rocket development programmes; (3) experience in building, launching and communicating with satellites in space; (4) a gradual improvement of the knowledge of the space environment; (5) electric power supplies which draw power from either the sun or nuclear or chemical fuels; (6) low noise receivers; (7) techniques for sensing and controlling vehicles in space; and (8) ground tracking equipment with high-speed computers.[3]

While the new communication revolution has made possible the transmission of information instantaneously and in abundance across national and cultural boundaries, and the growth potential of this revolution seems to have no end in sight, it has divided the people of the world into two groups — those who have the technology and those who do not — bringing in its wake many political, economic, technological and cultural problems.

Although the same technology can be used equally by the most developed and the most backward countries for conveying information and for advancing society, the unequal distribution of technical feasibility has resulted in the evolution of an information society in some countries, while in others it has made decision-makers more aware of the need to use this technology as a precursor to an industrial society. It has also made the developing countries aware of the urgent need for an industrial revolution in their countries.

The technological imperative

Constituting about two-thirds of the world, the developing countries are like bullock carts competing with modern lorries on a level motorway. The gap between the industrially developed and the Third and Fourth Worlds shows no signs of narrowing; rather, it is widening, and the lessons of the 1960s and 1970s show that technology imported from the industrial countries has led to distorted and disparate patterns of use and distribution of wealth in the less developed countries.

This, however, does not mean that the technology is obsolete or unsuited to bring about much needed change in the Third World. The issue is one of the transfer of appropriate technology, and the question concerns the adequacy of the latest technology to solve the problems of developing countries. Historically, the transfer of technology has been taking place for hundreds of years. The political, educational, economic and urban systems of today have all developed in the styles of the mother countries during colonial times. What developing countries aspire to today is a result of the colonial tradition. The structures and institutions in the developing countries are the remnants of colonial rule, whether in government, education or technology. Many developing countries have as their 'lingua franca' the language of the mother country. Even the assumption that poverty is associated with primitive technology and traditional values is an imported idea, and technology tends to be seen as a tool or a physical process.

In fact, technology *has* been present in the developing countries, although not as we identify it. Simple methods of increasing agricultural output by using different seeds, ploughs or indigenously produced handlooms can increase productivity and quality; folk media such as drums and wandering minstrels also exist, traditional yet efficient conveyors of the development message. These are not the capital-intensive methods based on economies of scale that are

known to us as 'modern technological innovations', however; while
these methods meet the peculiar individual requirements of the
developing countries, they cannot compete with modern technology
in terms of output, capability or speed.

Hence, the technological imperative. No longer can the poorer
countries depend solely on indigenous methods to improve productivity and promote economic development. Speed of development is
critical, and modern technology enables a quantum leap from a poor
society to a modern, sophisticated one. More particularly, communication technology is seen to bridge the gap between rich and poor,
city and village, educated and illiterate.

To achieve this, the new nations need the new technology. It is
available in the developed countries, and therefore the issue of the
transfer of technology assumes importance. 'Technology' here refers
to the systematic application of collective human rationality to the
solution of problems. What has to be transferred is not simply
machines or knowledge, but a collection of ideas, attitudes, values
and institutions; social, cultural and political structures.[4] Technology
transfer has always been seen to refer to technology of the capital-
intensive, sophisticated kind, without regard to social effects; to the
'know-how', that is, to knowledge and management systems,
sometimes without enough attention to the relevance or impact of
these techniques upon the socioeconomic and cultural fabric of the
developing countries. This is where the problem lies, and the introduction of these technologies causes an upheaval in the societies,
raising cultural and other crises, both negative and positive.

Let us take the case of communication technology. Essentially, the
use of this technology is no different from the use of industrial know-
how, but it has become the storm centre of much heated debate in the
world. There are two major components in using communication
technology: hardware and software.

Hardware
The present stage of information transmission in the more industrialized countries consists of high-cost, capital-intensive, labour-
saving devices based on the satellite and the computer. Assuming
that a decision has been made to use the most modern media available, the less developed country must, in reality, provide for two
systems, one based on the satellite and the other on the ground. The
first requires high initial investments in finances and know-how, skills
that have to be borrowed or purchased from the industrial nations.
Further, the receiving nation must be in a position to build and
operate the terrestrial facilities such as ground stations, distribution
and maintenance networks or receivers and microwave links. This

must be done in the face of the high costs of television transmission, the limited distribution of home receivers and the allocation of scarce resources.

The second system, required as a back-up to the satellites, is the ground system, based on microwave and other cable links. This is the more expensive network, but imagine the irony of putting all one's eggs in the satellite basket and having the satellite fail in its primary purpose owing to some technical error — as happened in the case of INSAT-IA or PALAPA, the Indian and Indonesian satellites.

The problem with the purchase of modern communication technology is that no two systems are compatible. It is not possible to purchase the ground facilities from one country and the launching facilities and satellite from another to reduce costs. A pattern of dependence is built up, and the poor nation must turn to one of the industrialized nations for all its facilities, spare parts, servicing, computer systems and so on. A package deal is arrived at, and unscrupulous business practitioners take advantage of the developing countries' technological naïvety, using these countries as dumping grounds for obsolete and defective technology.

Another problem is ensuring that technology is selected according to 'real need' rather than other criteria.[5] A nation needs a strong educational base of its own, but is it necessary to have computer-assisted instruction or colour transmission facilities in time to televise live some prestigious event? Is it merely a question of keeping up with the neighbours rather than making some hard decisions relating to the fulfilment of basic human needs at the village level?

What *would* be appropriate technology in terms of hardware? Pool[6] has suggested that, for a telecommunication system to serve less developed countries, it must first of all be cheap. It must also operate even in the absence of elaborate infrastructures such as stable electric current, microwave, cable networks and a smoothly functioning telephone service. Finally, it must link a developing country at its will to any possible source of data, not just to data bases in a favoured metropolis.

A tall order. But not impossible. To some extent, conventional systems, such as low-power localized radio stations, rural newspapers, community television sets, super 8mm film and mobile audiovisual vans, can do the job. These 'little media'[7] are more intimate; they are rich in possible variety, readily available, and relished by different age groups; they have a greater potential for instant feedback and are theme carriers of tradition. With their potential for operating outside soundproof studios, the new mobile 'mini-media', using simple and indigenous techniques, have the capability of linking the population with sophisticated technology.

Another method of employing the latest technology is to make use of the satellite facilities of another country by leasing a satellite for a given period of time, as in the SITE experiment, and preparing all the terrestrial hardware in the user-country. This permits the creation of a certain compulsory level of self-reliance which the developing country achieves, thus taking the first step in bridging the technological gap.

It is with the hardware facilities that infrastructural bases are constructed, and it is possible to take clear-cut decisions in the selection of hardware. But a more important and frequently neglected and misunderstood area is that of communication software, and it is here that the controversy between the industrialized centres and the developing countries lies.

Software

A very lively and often acrimonious debate has centred around the issue of communication software — What are the contents of the message? What is the purpose of such contents? And what is its net social effect? To date, less attention has been paid to software, and technology has often been discussed with little regard to the particular social and cultural milieu of communication.

Communication scholars in the developing nations have been advising development planners for some time now to pay close attention to the media. Other social scientists have been warning against the socially adverse effect of the media, which they feel, given the media's present form and content, are delivering messages and values antithetical to the values of the developing countries and are thus doing a very great disservice to 'authentic development'.[8]

There is little doubt as to how decision-makers of developing countries perceive the role of communication in development. The media, particularly radio and television, are the first institutions to be seized during periods of political instability or *coups d'état*. The introduction of television, whether by governments, to keep peace or further national integration or cohesion, or by private entrepreneurs to further their own interests, has often taken place for reasons not equated with development; yet media are recognized as vital tools by planners in the process of transmitting developmental messages to urban and rural populations alike. Rarely does a meeting take place where this view is not expressed at national and international levels.

Imported technology, particularly software such as packaged programmes, carries with it the built-in social and cultural biases of the exporting country. Predominantly Western in orientation, it has been prepared for the informational, educational and entertainment needs of Western audiences. To purchase such programmes and show them to audiences in the Third World is essentially to introduce them to a culture and society alien to their own in terms of practices and values. While it may be argued that development requires a change in outlook and attitude, many ask if the Protestant ethic and Western culture is the change desired.

Further, among the most fundamental of problems in developing countries is that of access and availability of technology. The elites and urbanites have greater access than those really in need of valuable information, thereby creating a new division of society into the have's and the have-not's — a national reflection of an international order. National politics and barriers to the full exploitation of modern technology are as much technological and institutional as social. Controlling the media technology and content, it is very easy for the urban, elite decision-maker in the capital to make the technology meet the needs of his own class. The priority of issues is altered accordingly.

Utilization of the new technology depends upon quality, timeliness and relevance. Information and technology with specific uses cease to be a resource and become a cost rather than a benefit. Because modern technology is expensive, capital-intensive and difficult to maintain, it is all the more essential that it be used for clear-cut developmental purposes.

Recognition and understanding of the policy options by decision-makers should include an understanding of the needs, circumstances and abilities of the users, so that the content of these technologies can be geared to meeting these needs. One effective method of doing this is by seeking the involvement and participation of the users of the technology. For example, if a telephone or television is installed in a village, the villagers can be involved in the construction of the building for the telephone exchange or housing for the television set.

The emphasis in technology software must shift from the technology itself to the user, and to the character and performance of existing infrastructure, before selection and developmental decisions are made. No single technology is the most appropriate, but the degree to which they can meet certain conditions determines their usefulness.[9] These conditions are (1) the requirement of the socio-economic milieu; (2) optimal use of local materials, personnel and financing; (3) job creation; and (4) lower cost. Concurrently, planners must look for control by people at the grassroots, a human scale of operation, environmental protection, and less dependency on external products. Let us look at the Indian experience to determine the extent to which a developing country has used technology without external dependence.

The Indian experience

Not all developing countries can make decisions which allow for the correct use of modern technology in development. The extent of their independence in decision-making, clear-cut policy goals, objectives and implementation, levels of technological competence, raw materials, indigenous capital and other factors relating to the audiences and to the ideological framework determine the extent of the nation's ability to use modern technology.

India has been a testing ground for many experiments, and more recently has been a pioneer in the use of modern communication technology for developmental purposes. If technology is knowledge or know-how, then the entire urban social system has its roots in the colonial heritage of Britain. From transport and communication links to the educational structure and the ideals of the urban Indian for a career in the civil service, all are connected with technologies brought to India by the British and left behind in the form of structures, institutions, practices, standards and motivational desires. India, perhaps, is one example of the thoughtless transplantation of institutions and culture and norms with partially relevant technologies which has led to a self-generating and self-perpetuating urban elite who conceived, designed and executed in true bureaucratic fashion.

It was only in the late 1960s and the 1970s and 1980s that scholars, technocrats and researchers began to look seriously at the technology of the developed countries. The lessons of the 1960s showed that Western technology was not necessarily applicable to the solution of India's many problems. The pattern was to borrow high-cost technology, acquire the management and get direction in research and development that was relevant only for the industrial cities. Technology appropriate to the satisfaction of basic human needs at the village level, such as how to run a cooperative, a public sector enterprise, rural development or banking schemes for villages, did not exist, nor did the means of rapidly transmitting timely information to rural India.

Examination showed that the growth of technology, especially in communication, has been haphazard. The ever-increasing costs of development in conventional media suggested that alternative methods of communication be found to reach the diverse, multilingual and fragmented population. The concerns of Indian leaders also centred around the issues of national integration in a multi-cultural society, where the centripetal forces tend to tear the country apart.

The alternative media that were used to reach rural audiences were those called 'little media'[10] — mobile vans with audiovisual packages; folk media and interpersonal interaction techniques; change agents and opinion leaders with indigenous ways of communicating to the vast population through localized pictures or symbols, wall posters, folk songs and drama. Effective media, but slow.

Little media are not enough when the task of reaching the people is monumental, and modern technology provides greater and more flexible ways of reaching audiences, although the danger of built-in dependency is high and the cost is prohibitive. A mix has to be arrived at which is going to bring the maximum benefit at minimum cost. Hence satellite technology.

The decisions taken by the Indian government and the experiments conducted by it all point to a clear-cut policy which, in spite of having no written guidelines, shows not only the Indian conception of the role of satellite technology but also policies related to the idea of self-reliance and the fear of dependency and cultural imperialism. In discussing the Indian experiments, we are concerned with the use of television via satellite for developmental purposes.

India started space research very modestly under the guidance of Dr Vikram Sarabhai in the late 1960s. At that time, television was present on an experimental basis in the capital. The first Experimental Satellite Communication Earth Station (ESCES) was established in 1965 and became operational in 1967. The push was on, and by 1975 India entered the space age by launching an indigenously designed and fabricated satellite, 'Aryabhata', from the USSR. Since then, six satellites have been launched by India, using US, Soviet and French launch facilities. India has also been developing its own capabilities from Sriharikota in the southern part of India, and the launch of Rohini from Indian launch facilities is no small achievement by any standards, let alone for a developing country.

The first experiments in satellite utilization for community education were conducted with NASA's ATS-6 satellite, which was positioned over India for one year in 1975–76. A quantum leap from zero to satellite, the Satellite Instructional Television Experiment (SITE) is among the most advanced and possibly the largest experiment in human communication ever carried out. Conducted in six clusters in six states, SITE encompassed 2,330 villages in varying degrees of backwardness. Television sets were installed for a direct reception system using 3m chicken mesh parabolic antennae. Programmes were telecast every morning and evening from Ahmedabad, with a capacity of one video and two audio channels. Divided into three subject areas — news, educational and recreational — the programmes were targeted for three types of audience: children of school-going age but not in school, pupils in elementary schools in rural areas, and illiterate and semi-literate adults.

While the findings of the micro-level evaluation and analyses were many, certain major conclusions bear special mention. First, satellites can be used to transmit information on agriculture, education, family planning and health to large numbers of people from different linguistic and ethnic backgrounds.[11] The experiment also proved that a satellite can be used to decentralize the production and transmission of information. More importantly, it showed that the use of foreign satellites did not necessarily mean dependence. Except for the satellite itself, all other infrastructure, from ground stations, distribution and maintenance of sets to the supply of materials in terms of hardware and the production and evaluation of software, was indigenously produced, enabling self-reliance to be attained in certain crucial elements in communication.

The SITE collaboration was followed by the Satellite Telecommunication Experiment Project (STEP), conducted by India and using the Franco–German satellite 'Symphonie' in 1977–79. The objective of the experiments was to develop and test indigenous competency and expertise in the hardware aspects of satellite technology.

The latest major experiment in direct broadcast systems, and the sequel to SITE, STEP and APPLE, is the INSAT (Indian Satellite) system, providing for the world's first geostationary satellite combining telecommunications, direct television broadcasting and metereological services.

INSAT IA, which was launched from the US launch facilities at Cape Canaveral on 10 April 1982, was delayed for more than one year, and the 1,090 kg multipurpose satellite caused some flutter and panic when the solar panel did not open fully for more than two weeks following the launch. The INSAT IA system failed, but in its wake was launched the INSAT IB, via the space shuttle. This satellite is operating successfully and forms the technological basis for use in such varied fields as developmental communication, remote sensing, monitoring weather conditions and telecommunications.

There is little argument in India as to whether modern communication technology can be used as appropriate technology for a developing nation. The government of Prime Minister Rajiv Gandhi has placed its emphasis on the promotion of the technological revolution by giving encouragement to the electronics industry to grow and develop in an atmosphere of competition. The projections are that, by the beginning of the twenty-first century, India, through the use of technology, will make the leap. It should then be a medium-level industrial power and should achieve complete self-sufficiency in agricultural production. Satellites and computers will be India's partners in this progress.[12]

The leap forward cannot be achieved easily. More important than the technological changes it brings to society are the consequences upon society, upon the polity and upon various aspects of human life, and it is these changes that call for greater study and concern. For even in India, modern technology has changed the dimensions of human life and irrevocably altered the rules of the game.

Societal impact

In today's world, the politics of power are also the politics of technology. The nations which can own, operate and control sophisticated satellites command the destinies of the world. The Star Wars programme epitomizes this power. No longer can the national sovereignty of a nation be determined by its ability to defend its territorial integrity against foreign invasion.

There are no national boundaries for technology. The politics of space are an extension of the politics of earth. To date, the two super-powers have largely determined how many satellites would be launched and for what purpose. The industrial nations have determined the pace of technological development, and the content of communication. In so far as they have developed incompatible systems, they have ensured that the countries purchasing technology remain dependent upon them for spares, maintenance, tracking and control and software, thus altering the colour of dependency while retaining its nature.

Several issues are crucial to the new order, for example, the availability of parking places for satellites in space at an altitude of 23,000 miles where there is capacity for only 180 satellites. The allotment of these places proved to be a major issue at the World Administrative Radio Conference (WARC) in 1979, where the concern of the developing countries that their future growth would be stunted if places were not reserved was most seriously expressed, a view not shared by the technologically superior nations.

A second major issue in the new order concerns the problem of ownership, operation and control of the satellites in space. The technology for the manufacture, launching, tracking, repair and maintenance of satellites is available only in the developed countries, with the notable exception of India. To share this technology means to share power, and no nation wishes to dilute its power potential.

Another critical aspect of the new order is the development of the technology to broadcast directly from space to home receivers, that is, to the direct broadcasting systems. This capacity makes a mockery of national boundaries, because the powerful satellite can be used to beam signals to receivers in another country directly. The ability to broadcast across national frontiers has been a concern for many decades, but nations are now beginning to take action. As even some

LIBRARY ST. MARY'S COLLEGE

developed nations such as Canada and Australia have found themselves threatened by this awesome power, they are passing legislation to protect their airwaves and the content of programming. To the developing nations, the threat of direct broadcasting is even more serious, particularly as concerns in these nations centre around issues of nation-building while the content of Western media is at variance with the values of the developing country, creating cultural imperialism.

The policy options relating to the use of technology are factors which require serious attention. The problems of development lie in the needs and circumstances of the users of technology and the need to be identified and understood before decisions relating to the choice of technology are made. Decisions about use and other investments must encompass the interests and skills of both the high-level technocrat and the low-level user with an emphasis on self-help and participation. Unfortunately, political and institutional considerations have often intervened to compromise the effectiveness of technology in delivering the goals.[13] The selection of technology, and the political motivations behind its implementation, have usually rendered the technology inappropriate.

Finally, access to the technology of the developed nations is fraught with political implications. Space research and other innovations of the past decade have been spillovers from defence programmes, and donor nations of technology are ever watchful of the causes for which the user-nation seeks technology. The capacity to launch satellites is also seen as the capacity to launch ballistic missiles, and donor nations do not want a proliferation of this capability. As for the powerful nations, we can only guess at the number of satellites being used for monitoring and spying on rival countries. For non-technological reasons, both nations and multinational corporations guard their secrets very carefully.

Technology has made an impact on both individuals and society. The important factor to remember is that in contemporary international communication the basic purpose is to keep before the individual and the nation the awareness that they have the freedom to interact and to choose. In reality, this choice is lost. Technology is always talked of in economic and engineering terms, without the social and cultural milieu in view; and it has always been of a capital-intensive kind, without much regard to the social effects or its appropriateness. When technology is introduced, people have to be trained. Training is usually taken up as an afterthought, when the equipment is lying unused in institutions.

More significantly, the population needs to be made aware of the potential of the technology. Workers should not view modern technology as a threat to their jobs. They have to be made to understand that the technology is brought in not to replace them, but to make their work easier. This climate is rarely created; thus the decisions to use technology are viewed with suspicion and anger, rather than with a healthy curiosity or a willingness to adapt.

The effects of technology are evident everywhere. At its most simple level, technology such as the communication satellite has rapidly increased the awareness level of rural and urban folk alike. Satellite communication has been the magic multiplier, reaching out to areas hitherto unreachable. Both studies of the SITE experience and others done in rural areas have shown that information, when carefully planned and prepared and when linked to the real needs of rural folk, has been welcomed.[14] Television exposure has helped in the adoption of innovations, especially when only an alteration to existing practices was involved, rather than innovations. On the whole, the effect upon development has been positive; audiences do learn from the media, although the nature of this learning is of greater general awareness rather than specific impact related to programme content.

The unequal pace of technological development between the urban and rural areas, where the urban areas are both the producers and the beneficiaries of technology, has increased inequalities between urban centres and the rural periphery. The overall purpose of technological progress should be to produce a more egalitarian society. But today's technology is itself class-oriented, tending to increase divisions between social groups. The gap between the information-rich and information-poor has widened, contrary to the expectations of the planners; and the hopes that technology would enable the growth of a more egalitarian society have not been met. In a situation where the requirements of the developing nations are so important, such a tendency is dangerous. It must be noted that the hardware does have a propensity for equalizing the disparity between the urban and the rural; it is the software that has a tendency to widen the already existing divisions.

These divisions, with power in the hands of an urban elite which controls the technology and the rural population on the receiving end, have their own repercussions. There is no equality of access to and availability of technology. Urban areas are saturated with technology, and rural areas are barren.

This raises the final philosophical issues. Are we now talking about the individual or the greater social good? If new technology is to be used to give the individual an awareness of the opportunities of a better life, what are these opportunities? Do the values of media freedom, individual choice and Protestant ethic enable us to meet the requirements and demands of the vast majority of our socially weakened communities? What is the kind of development we want — development in material wealth or development of the human spirit? Is technology the way to achieve our goals rapidly?

If, indeed, we accept that we want development and feel that technology plays an important role in this process, then the philosophical and ideological questions become vitally important. Are we prepared for the social upheavals that will result, and are we willing to pay the social price for such development? And at what stage are we able or prepared to impose control on the effects of the technological revolution? In fact, can we control it at all?

If development is indeed our goal, we have no option but to use technology. But to succeed in our objective, there has to be a strong ideological base and the single-minded, ruthless implementation that comes with it. Perhaps what is required is the sacrifice of the individual for the larger social good over at least one generation, and very clear-cut attempts to maintain cultural identity and national cohesion in the face of a universal homogenization not consonant with the concepts of sovereignty, self-reliance and independence. We must master the technology, not become its slaves.

Notes

1. Majid F. Tehranian, V. Hakimzadeh and L. Marcelle, *Communications Policy for National Development: A Comparative Perspective*. London: Routledge and Kegan Paul, 1977.

2. *ibid*.

3. G.E. Mueller and E.R. Spangler, *Communication Satellites*. New York: John Wiley, 1964.

4. Elihu Katz and G. Wedell, *Broadcasting in the Third World: Promise and Performance*. London: Macmillan, 1978.

5. Anthony Smith, *The Geopolitics of Information*. London: Faber and Faber, 1980.

6. Ithiel de Sola Pool, 'Direct Broadcast Satellites and the Integrity of National Culture', in Kaarle Nordenstreng and Herbert I. Schiller, *National Sovereignty and International Communication*. Norwood, NJ: Ablex Publishing, 1979.

7. Wilbur Schramm, *Big Media, Little Media, Tools and Technology for Instruction*. Beverly Hills: Sage, 1977.

8. Katz and Wedell, op. cit.

9. Denis Goulet, *The Uncertain Promise, Value Conflicts in Technology Transfer*. New York: IDDC, 1977.

10. See John L. Mitchell, 'Communication and Appropriate Technology', *Media Asia*, 1976, 3(4):224–8. See also Schramm, op. cit.

11. Binod C. Agrawal, *Television Comes to Villages: An Evaluation of SITE*. Ahmedabad: Space Applications Centre, 1978.

12. *The Telegraph*, 6 July 1985.

13. John L. Mitchell, 'The Appropriateness of Satellite Communication for the Third World', *Media Asia*, 1978, 5(2):90–102.

14. *The SITE Experience*. Paris: UNESCO, 1983.

7

Communication as if people matter: the challenge of alternative communication

Mina M. Ramirez

Various academic disciplines today emphasize the specifically human in their respective subjects. There is a call for 'economics as if people mattered',[1] a move for a 'more humanistic psychology', and another for a 'more humanistic sociology'.[2] Disciplines which are understood to deal with human beings now have to challenge professionals to 'make people matter' in their respective fields. And communication is no exception.

What is the world context in which a consideration of the human is being questioned? Are persons about to be engulfed by forces that will dehumanize them? Is life, meaningful life that is, being put to the test? And if so, what world forces are referred to by critical, reflective persons who plead for a more human approach to supposedly humanistic social involvements and projects?

A situational analysis reveals that there is a crisis of values, a moral crisis affecting both nations and peoples. Like a poisonous gas, it penetrates the tissues of every so-called human project and slowly kills whatever is noble in the human spirit.

From a moral, social and spiritual perspective, this 'poisonous gas' is called, respectively, 'organized greed',[3] 'situations of injustice',[4] and 'social sin'.[5] The result is senselessness and gross materialism, sometimes justified by a spiritualism that exploits the religious sentiments or 'yearnings' of people.[6] Through science and technology, the race for profit and power has assumed overwhelming proportions. It almost appears that the global crisis, humanly speaking, has reached a point of no return.

Global dimensions of the reality

The International Economic Order[7]
Many people of the Third World suffer from poverty with all its consequences — malnutrition, poor health, lack of education, substandard housing, and a life below the level of subsistence.

This poverty in the Third World has its roots in an international economic order in which the profit motive in the First World — and among the powerful economic and political elites of the Third World countries — overrides all considerations that see the common good of the great majority as primary. This economic order reinforces imbalances between the developed and the developing countries and between the rich and the poor in each country.

Capitalism, which has conquered practically the whole world, even so-called socialist countries, is further reinforced by a trilateral arrangement between the USA, Western Europe and Japan.[8] From these regions has emerged a trilateral commission, supposedly to spread enlightened capitalism in the world. This commission has been instrumental in introducing development packages into the Third World with the assistance of international financial inter-mediaries such as the World Bank and the International Monetary Fund. Hence, in Asian countries one finds the same development schemes throughout — export processing zones, international tourism and agri-business.[9]

It is well known that these development schemes have only diverted local capital, needed for rural development, to the building of infrastructure like roads and hotels. Unemployment has not been resolved. On the contrary, because of the growth of agri-business, as in the case of the Philippines, a significant number of families have been driven away from their land to give way to multinational corpo-rations. International (foreign) reserves or a favourable balance of payments have not been achieved. The fact is that, as these activities are enhanced, the countries go deeper into debt. The local elite may profit much from an economy that is export-oriented, but this, more often than not, is at the expense of the welfare of the great majority of families in the rural as well as in the urban areas.

The International Political Order[10]
With a world economy that is based merely on profit, political stability in the Third World becomes a primary consideration to enable business which is oriented to the world market to operate without interference from labour movements that may protest against low wages. Policies such as this are a result of the National Security Ideology.

The National Security Ideology tends to make human development objectives secondary. Thus, some countries in Asia spend much more for defence than for health and education, while powerful countries unreservedly accumulate arms and nuclear weapons. On the arms race, especially among powerful countries, Dwight Eisenhower made this statement: 'Every gun that is made, every warship launched, every rocket fired signifies, in a final sense, a theft from those who hunger and are not fed, from those who are cold and are not clothed.' The Brandt Commission (1980) likewise remarked that, 'The build-up of arms in large parts of the Third World itself causes growing instability and undermines development. . . . More arms do not make mankind safe, only poorer.'

As a result of this national security orientation, it is the state that has become the centre of governments' preoccupations, and not the person or the collectivity of persons called 'the nation'. At present, no developing country is truly sovereign, and the great majority of the poor in various countries have become powerless.

The National Security Ideology, through the promotion of totalitarian governments and militarization, fulfils yet another function. It acts as a controlling element to stabilize a situation of 'unjust peace'. This situation curtails the free expression of protest among economically powerless people and the basic freedom to gain some collective power through organization. The stabilization process is needed for the maintenance and growth of multinational corporations and their development schemes. But these do not effect a more equitable distribution of resources, services and decision-making power. On the contrary, they have caused an urban growth through internal migration from the countryside to the city.

While dimensions of global economic and political trends influence the national government's choice of a development model whose effects run counter to people's aspirations, it is also true that in the Third World, especially in the Asian region, the people still have to be liberated from discrimination of all forms, based on age, sex, class, race, language, culture, religion, political ideology and feudalistic structures.

The International Information and Communication Order[11]
The most subtle form of domination is in the realm of the International Information and Communication Order. In this area there is a monopoly of information and communication by the First World countries and/or by the rich in the Third World countries, and negligence in the promotion of such human values as cultural integrity, self-reliance, participation, autonomy, empathy, responsibility, diversity and plurality, a sense of community and spirituality.

The transnational corporations and their political partners maintain control of all forms of media. This promotes attitudes of materialism and consumerism.

Colonialism: a social malady
Within this world order, the great majority of Third World peoples do not understand the devastating consequences of a political, economic and cultural imperialism that curtails their growth as

persons, as communities and as nations. Through a monopoly of information and communication, the present political and economic system has succeeded in desensitizing minds and hearts to the quality of life being perpetrated by a capitalistic system which urges people to want more and more, to buy more and more, despite limited resources. Having, not being; the package, not the product; big is beautiful, big is expensive — these are values which in their gross materialism dehumanize.

The social actors in this drama are the monopolizers of power. They are the elites of the transnational corporations, world powers, and their counterparts in the Third World. They sedate the modernizing elite — the leaders of institutions — with their images of a world being secured by a balance of nuclear weapons and an industrialized economy which has exploited natural resources to the limits. Unwittingly, human involvements and projects become poisoned by the value of accumulation of profit.

But how did this accumulation game start? A theologian, Brendan Lovett,[12] states that it started not with the industrial revolution but further back — five hundred years back. He cites an incredible novel entitled *The Name of the Rose*, by Umberto Eco, in which the author talks about a crucifix in a church. In this crucifix Christ has one hand nailed to the cross and the other hand holding on to a bag of money, to show that being a Christian is quite compatible with the accumulation of capital. It seems, according to Lovett, that in canonical tracts and works of the fourteenth and fifteenth centuries the laity were exhorted not just to work, but to work to accumulate: 'The reason the Church is teaching this is because the Church itself has got a hard conscience about having gone into the accumulation game in a big way.' Colonialism of the fifteenth and sixteenth centuries has been an integral part of this accumulation game. And it is this value that has penetrated into the marrow of the economic and political system.

Each Third World country has its own unique experience of this colonialism.

The Philippines: a case in point

The accumulation game exemplified in subjugating peoples has a model in the Philippines. Few countries feel the devastating consequences of a colonial history more intensely than the socially aware Filipinos. Although still a minority, they constitute a movement capable of finally realizing a search for counter-values which move people to create for themselves alternative structures in different institutional spheres. The process may be long. But the various initiatives offer some hope.[13]

What have these socially aware groups finally realized? That their culture has been suppressed by a long colonial history; that colonialism and neo-colonialism have seriously impaired the future development and enrichment of their languages; that their own religious symbols have been rejected; their original script, destroyed. Filipinos have been taught that their own culture — language, art, drama, rituals and even their attitude towards women,[14] which, from the perspective of today, was quite progressive — is inferior to the European and North American culture. In so doing, the Filipinos were made to reject themselves.

In this colonial history, the missionary schools — Catholic and Protestant alike — were instrumental in perpetrating a rejection of indigenous culture. It is within this context that the late Jesuit historian of the Philippines, Horacio de la Costa, lamented, 'Why are all efforts for development becoming obstacles to development?' His question pointed to the phenomenon of a great number of Catholic schools where students learned to speak very fine English but could not communicate with the average Filipino, especially with the 70 percent living in the rural areas.

One indication of the suppression of a people's culture is the dual cultural system operating in a country. Because all institutions — political, economic, education and religious — have been imposed from without, the result is that every institution has an *informal* system that is more alive than the formal one. The informal system is a way of coping with the formal institutions which the people do not feel at home with. Such institutions do not seem to offer the great majority of people the quality of life they aspire to.

Thus, in all spheres of institutional life, an informal system has evolved that caters to the needs of the masses. This is particularly visible in cities, where modernization processes have not been matched by human and social development in the rural areas. Understandably, hordes of people victimized by unequal development and mass media images of the 'good life' have been persuaded to migrate to the cities. There they have devised social mechanisms both to survive and to serve the interests of others of their kind. In the informal economy, one finds children and adults who engage in vending food, cigarettes, newspapers and the like, or in rendering services such as shoeshining, car-watching and touting for passengers for 'jeepneys' (small transportation vehicles). To allow the political machinery to run smoothly, there are 'fixers' (those who for a fee arrange for papers to be processed); and others who, like bureaucratic middlemen, are auxiliaries to the people in office. These auxiliaries share a percentage of their service fees and commissions with the rank-and-file government employees (who are often paid very low wages). Similarly, policemen take their share from the tips of the jeepney-touts.

The educational and religious institutions have not been free from the activities associated with the informal sector. Since teachers in the Philippines are the lowest paid professionals in the country, it is seldom that a teacher can live by teaching alone. The practice of teachers selling all types of commodities in school is rampant. There are those who are given the name of educational counsellors, a euphemistic term to identify teachers who sell encyclopaedias to students for a commission. Selling religious images like the Santo Niño (the image of the Boy Jesus), considered as a wonder worker, has also become very popular. Indeed, the struggle for survival in an economy, polity, education, and religion with Western cultural presuppositions becomes symbolized by the workings of an informal sector.

According to such presuppositions, these informal arrangements are dysfunctional to the system that has been derived from the West; for the system is supposed to create order, discipline and maximum efficiency.

It seems quite clear that industrialization and bureaucratization have not created a spin-off that can offer the people a general sense of well-being. On the contrary, to be able to survive in an inadequate system, the people have had to create an informal sector that can respond, even if only minimally, to their basic needs.

Colonialism and neo-colonialism are a social malady. They have compelled people to reject themselves, to lose their identity, and to want what their Western counterparts want. Not having acquired a self-identity, they have been thrown into a technological and industrial maze whose meanings they have not sorted out for themselves. Except for those few who are aware of the assumptions and presuppositions of the life that is being offered to them, the great majority have uncritically accepted what is being communicated to them by Western powers working hand in hand with the local political and economic elites who benefit most from the structures created.

A suppressed culture is an uncommunicative culture. This kind of suppression simply means that people have not yet told their stories. The dominant culture — that which is promoted by television, radio, popular magazines and newspapers, and is symbolized in institutional life — has profoundly destroyed the capacity of a people to react and to protest against domination, manipulation and exploitation.

The most subtle form of dominance is that of the mind. The most detestable sort of dependence is not material but spiritual: people have lost the power to think critically for themselves.[15] The moment people lose this power, they are not able to communicate. They can only ape.

In the context of this reality, it is imperative to challenge people to be aware of the social trauma wrought by colonialization and the devastating consequences of neo-colonialism in this century. The challenge of alternative communication is one posed to the modernizing elite — leaders of institutions — to take stock of the rich experiences of people. They should act like midwives to bring to birth the deepest feelings, anxieties, dreams and aspirations of the people who have become marginalized, so that they can realize their potential, the richness of their art forms, and their ideas about the meaning of life.

Alternative communication

Communication qualifies human life. Through communication, persons maintain contact with their environment. Communication enables human beings to act, adapt and transmit resources for survival. Through communication, culture is created which continually adapts 'action repertories' and other survival resources and passes them on. Life continues only because of communication which creates cultures, of which language becomes the foundation. Institutions are the superstructures of culture. They evolve from the culture through the mediation of communication processes.[16]

But what happens when culture has been suppressed and has become uncommunicative? What happens when a dominant culture has imposed on a people its own values, norms and institutions?

Colonialism and neo-colonialism have imposed institutions and a culture that have prevented the people of Third World countries from communicating. The result is a dual culture, a dual institutional system. From the perspective of the dominant culture, the cultural and institutional system which operates among the people is a deviation from the 'official' system. From the perspective of the people, the dominant culture and institutional system does not respond adequately to their real and basic needs.

A people culturally alienated should be liberated from the dehumanizing effects of colonialism and neo-colonialism. This can be initiated by promoting communication processes which will make people realize the root reasons why the dominant culture and institutions do not respond to their real needs. Equally important is that people discover in their own way the context in which their lives have been trapped, their coping mechanisms, and the creativity by which they strive to survive materially, emotionally and spiritually. How do they maintain their humanness within the social limitations in which they have been caught? In other words, an authentic collective self-understanding has to take place before a people can develop its ideas on how to integrate the informal with the formal systems.

In the Third World today, there is a growing movement of people who are beginning to tell their stories. The taken-for-granted reality perceived by the dominant culture as inferior is slowly surfacing through various communication approaches. These approaches are in the realm of participative research and group media. They in turn become the basis for action, organization and alternative institutions. The overall consequence of these alternative communication processes is a collective self-awareness on the part of groups that have been materially and culturally marginalized. The stories people tell may still be the vital link between the contemporary modern world and the traditional values of people. They may still be the mediating element that will humanize communication and institutions. Indeed, cultural identity is the springboard for people's self-confidence to develop and for people's rich potentials and inner cultural resources to resolve the large-scale forces that affect them. For people to be fully human, they should be able to define for themselves what general well-being is in the context of their experiences as persons, as communities and as nations.

It is worthwhile at this juncture to cite an example of the impact of the stories that people tell. These stories have the capacity to humanize their subjects as well as others who listen to them.

A beginner's model of alternative communication
A beginner's model of an alternative communication process is presented here. This involves students of a phenomenology class who, through a videotape production titled 'Celso and Cora', were able to speak with marginalized people from the streets of Manila.[17] The film is a documentary which caught fragments of the life of a couple, migrants from the provinces, who engaged in cigarette vending in one of the tourist areas in Manila.[18] The one-and-a-half hour film portrays the struggle of the couple to meet the basic needs of life — housing, employment and welfare services. The hazards of such a life are vividly depicted.

Ten cigarette vendors, mostly young people, with an elderly couple among them, were invited to view the film, which portrayed the hidden dimensions of life of people-in-the-streets. From life experiences spontaneously and candidly articulated by the cigarette vendors, the students listening to their stories identified the following themes:

— shared experience as spontaneous wisdom;
— work as a life-symbol;
— inventiveness in skills and networking;
— dialogical sincerity;
— supportive relationships;
— humour in crisis;
— confronting poverty with dignity;
— spirituality as responsible participation in the challenges of life.

One long story specifically demonstrated the tenacity with which a cigarette vendor coped with the hardships of city life. In ten years, this vendor had changed jobs 15 times and had married three times. Reflecting on his life, he saw the possibility of an organization of vendors in Manila's city streets. He realized what a great potential as a group or sector they could have, even as a tax resource for the government.

From the concrete facts of their life, the students who listened to the vendors discussed their insights into this specific reality. They saw the possibilities of a medium like the video film for stimulating people to tell their stories. They saw possibilities for participatory book publishing, by which the stories of people could be communicated to various institutional spheres for these to respond authentically to people's needs. They glimpsed the human qualities of a people trying to survive in a harsh environment and yet not giving up the hope of a better future.

These stories show how cigarette vendors have struggled to cope with institutions which hamper their attempts to live a more human life. In this struggle, they are continually creating informal ways of fulfilling their basic needs. The students (the future modernizing elite) were touched by the stories and made explicit their insights on the matter. One of them, Marissa Mantala, wrote:

> I cannot blame people who obstinately stay in the city despite the hazards posed by city life. They have to find the means to stay alive. In the city they find it easier to earn money because of the presence of odd jobs which are not possible in rural communities. It is no wonder then that government efforts to bring them back to the province are a failure. Rural development as envisaged by government authorities does not reflect the people's needs. Real development should bring about changes in access to economic opportunities. Only by access to economic opportunities in the rural areas can we prevent people from urban migration which will eventually lead to the lessening of similar problems in the urban centres.

Another student, Noel Valencia, made the following observations:

It is tempting for some to stop short in their consideration of 'Celso and Cora' and of the stories of the cigarette vendors and just simply romanticize about their situation, taking bits and pieces of gestures or conversations, examining these 'phenomenologically' and then saying, despite their abject poverty, they are still human after all. I believe it is most important to see and inquire about how Celso and Cora and other persons like them can transcend their poverty.

I believe that one aspect of people's self-project is transformative praxis which takes into consideration, as one sets about transcending one's reality, not only the subjective pole of being but also the objective pole of external society. To conceive of Celso and Cora transcending their situation, one should also conceive that the possibility of this rests in the changing of the material complex which determines them, and this can only be carried out in unity with the persons comprising their social class.

Communication as if people matter

A people who have been utterly disregarded in the interests of material accumulation by national and global powers should be given the chance to articulate and express their deepest human feelings about the realities of their life. This is the challenge of alternative communication. In contrast to the one-way information flow which is controlled by political and economic powers, alternative communication shifts its focus to the stories being told by the marginalized and exploited sectors of society. The negative social consequences of colonialism and neo-colonialism are deeply embedded in people. And the therapy for such a malady is the creation of a social climate for 'story-telling'.

It is high time that the policy-makers (including the technocrats) listened to the stories that people tell.

'Story-telling' could further be systematized. This would mean organizing and mobilizing each sector, particularly the most marginalized, towards democratic processes and leadership. These organizations may form pressure groups promoting a new self-consciousness — an awareness of the roots of their condition as well as the potentials for their own liberation. Each sector could be helped by sympathetic groups among the modernizing elite. Through movements such as these, the real needs of people are easily identified.

The people's stories could be channelled to a wider audience through mass media so that public opinion and positive institutional responses to people's needs may be formed and crystallized. Steps would have to be taken by various institutions to recognize and communicate the valuable contributions of the various organized sectors towards a more human life in society as a whole. In the last analysis, the establishment of a system of communication in which people matter entails the struggle of all sectors of society to obtain control of communication processes which can lead to collective understanding of human situations. Such an understanding, based on reality, action and reflection, is the basis for an alternative economic, political and communicative order. Such communication would pose a challenge to the great capacities which people have for personal, communal and societal transformation.

Appendix:

Transcript of the cigarette vendors' stories

What follows is some excerpts from the stories of the cigarette vendors, translated from tapes in the national language (Tagalog) into English. The discussions took place at the Asian Social Institute in May 1985.

Cigarette Vendor 1: The story of Celso and Cora is a fine story, but my story you still do not know.

Cigarette Vendor 2: The story is a fine one but mine is even more dramatic than the one shown.

Cigarette Vendor 3: For me it is a true story. For I also went through the same experiences. Once my child got sick with measles and I brought him to Philippine General Hospital. I was able to buy medicine only through my earnings as a cigarette vendor. I did not ask for help from anybody, not even from my parents, and I am proud of this.

Cigarette Vendor 4: I have three children and am 23 years old. I married in 1979. My wife is working. Formerly she was in a bakery. We met each other there. I was baking bread. She was selling bread. Since I was 10 years old, I worked in the bakery. I told the Chinese man, 'Boss, I'll work in your bakery as a cleaner.' 'All right', said the Chinese. My salary was 60 pesos (US$7.50) monthly. Whenever my Chinese boss was sitting in his office, I would get his book which contained all kinds of recipes for baking. For any mixture, the book would state how much sugar for how many sacks of flour, how much water and salt should be in the mixture. My boss once asked me, 'How did you learn this?' And I answered, 'Boss, I have gone to school.' Soon I was asked to be a master-baker ('maestro'[19]). I was able to bake muffins, cakes, even special birthday cakes. People asked me, 'How were you able to read?' My response was, 'I have brains. I can live anywhere.' It was in this bakery that I met my wife. I did not court my wife the way the others did. Seven other men used to take her out. I had to work because I still have brothers and sisters to support. My wife must have seen my sincerity to work. That was how she chose me. My wife is 27, a bit older than I am. By God's mercy, we are happy, not too many problems in married life. I never beat my wife. That is not a custom among us Visayans (*a major ethnic group in the Philippines*).

We can eat three times a day.

I transferred to cigarette vending because I was earning too little from the bakery. I asked my boss for an increase in wage. I told him that I needed this to support my wife and children. He was giving me 300 pesos (US$37.50) monthly with free food. But I still had to pay for transport. It just couldn't be. If my wife and children would get sick, what then? I told myself, I'll try to look for a decent job — a work with dignity. On average, I earn 50 pesos (US$6.25) a day as a cigarette vendor.

Cigarette Vendor 5: I am the first cigarette vendor on Taft Avenue. I am the president of our association. Now our association has weakened. It all started when policemen got into the habit of arbitrarily arresting cigarette vendors. When I was elected president, I used to collect 2 pesos (US$0.25) daily from each vendor. We were 15 at the start in this association. We increased to 25. When I couldn't sell cigarettes, I would sell peanuts. I would earn 50–80 pesos (US$6.25–$10.00). The maximum earning would be 100 pesos (US$12.50) daily.

When it rains, peanuts are very saleable. They keep the people warm. By noontime, the peanuts would be all sold out. I would make the trip from Cubao to Makati (about 10 km). I climb on buses to sell. I shout, 'Peanuts, peanuts, delicious, hard, crispy peanuts!'

I am a homosexual. I tell this to you so you know who I really am. At one time, I would sport jewelries while selling cigarettes. My brother who works in Manila Hotel objected to my selling cigarettes. 'You will be accused of being a snatcher', he warned me. 'Why,' I countered, 'Are all vendors considered thieves?'

I am the youngest. My other brothers and sisters are in the States. I am the only poor one in my family. Some professionals think we are downtrodden people, but they do not know that the lower-paid professionals earn only 1,500 pesos (US$187.50) a month; we could earn from cigarette vending 2,000 pesos (US$250) monthly. The professionals receive money every 15 days; we have money everyday. Moreover, we have no boss; we are our own bosses. We work anytime. We are free to decide how to use our time. We have the freedom to work, to sleep, to go out, to eat and do anything. We can buy whatever we like with our hard-earned money.

Here in Taft Avenue, we have plenty of fights. Some other group wants to sell in Taft Avenue. Sometimes they think that they can easily take over this street just because I am a homosexual. They want to harass and threaten me. But they fail to do so.

Along Taft Avenue, we do not sell at the same time. Some sell at night; others, during the day. For if we all sold at the same time, we would saturate the market. We would not earn much. Some are stationed near UN Avenue, others in Padre Faura St, others in Herran St, and still others in Vito Cruz St.

There are policemen who try to arrest us. When we get arrested, the association to which we contribute US$0.25 daily bails us out. Bail money is US$7.50. In the beginning, it was only US$3.75.

Cigarette Vendor 6: Street-vendors do a service. Look,if you are a jeepney driver or a passenger, you need not get out of the vehicle to buy a cigarette. The cigarette vendor approaches you; he even lights your cigarette.

Cigarette Vendor 7: One gets a feeling of satisfaction from cigarette vending, knowing that what one eats comes from the sweat of one's work. We do not mind the hardships we go through. . . .

The policemen do not know that we sell in order to earn money for our education. We would rather sell than do wrong. But what is terribly wrong is that the policemen arrest you for trying to earn a decent livelihood; while those who really steal are not caught. We borrow some capital in order to be able to sell cigarettes. From our little merchandise, the policemen would ask for one pack of Philip Morris. That might still be okay (we could still earn despite this practice) as long as this is not persistent. For when our merchandise is gone, we have to borrow again. This spells another problem. Why does government not give us the opportunity to earn money which prevents us from doing something wrong?

Cigarette Vendor 8: In our living quarters, we are required to pay 10,000 pesos (US$1,250) for a 20 square metre lot. We complained about this. If only the squatters would unite, we could declare that we really have nothing to pay. Our houses were demolished; we were transferred to another area and then the government demanded payment from us.

Cigarette Vendor 9: I should tell you how I became a cigarette vendor. Mine is a long story. I was born 17 April 1949. I am now 36 years old. I lived in a rural area in Leyte Island. We were fortunate to own some land but my parents did not care much for it. My father would rather go fishing. As a young man of 16 years, I was assigned to till the land. But I also studied. I used to invite my schoolmates to help me with the land. I did not have to pay them. In return, I should also help them with their land. Since my father was not interested in the land, I also lost interest in it. I felt I couldn't manage the land alone.

As a young man, I had my own dreams. I wanted to finish schooling. One night I overheard my grandfather saying, 'Jose (that is the name of my father), if I were you, I would not let the children study, because there are many persons who have completed their schooling as lawyers, teachers and engineers, and yet, till now, they haven't found work. Since your child knows how to read and write, let him just work on the land. After all, sons soon marry. And when they are married, they will not be able to contribute to your family.' Of course, I felt bad although I did not show my feelings. And sure enough, when I expressed to my father my desire to study, he said, 'Oh no, son, studies are not needed. Just work on the land.' I felt terribly hurt. So I said to myself, 'It might be better to leave the province and go to Manila.'

The opportunity to go to Manila occurred when some friends planned a trip to Manila. Arriving there, I took a job as a gardener at 28 pesos (US$3.50) a month. I couldn't stay long in this job. I was lonely. I always thought of my girlfriends. I remembered the happy times we had in the ship that sailed to Manila. When I felt like crying, I would go to the bathroom and cry profusely. After the third day, I went to Divisoria, a big public market. I went there to visit one of my friends. She was staying in a building. There she asked me to cook rice. And I told her how lonely I was as a gardener. From my friend's place, I walked and walked in Divisoria. I met another one of my girlfriends. In my joy, I embraced her. 'How are you?' she asked. 'Well here I am,' I said. 'I just have been in the house of one of our friends.' 'Well then,' the girl said, 'Daily you may visit me in school so that we can see each other. If my master would like to have a houseboy, I'll recommend you — so we could be together.' 'That's okay,' I quickly remarked.

However, I did not see her anymore. But I met another one of my girlfriends in the same school, one of the elderly ones, a girl of 28 years old. She asked me about my work. I told her I did not have a job. Then she said, 'I think it is best that you try a job in a bakery. One of my friends whose husband is in a bakery might need a helper.' 'Well, please do recommend me,' I pleaded. That same afternoon, I was accepted as a cleaner at the bakery. . . . My monthly pay was the measly amount of 25 pesos (US$3.25) a month. As a cleaner, I felt like an auto-mechanic. I was always full of ash. Every afternoon I would scrub the floor, rubbing off the sticky dough. The Chinese boss seemed pleased.

When another one of my province-mates joined me, the Chinese made me teach him my job as a cleaner. I was then promoted to be the helper of the master-baker ('maestro'). My only job was to follow his instructions. In the meantime I learned a lot about baking. Beer was very cheap at that time. One evening, I invited the 'maestro' to have a glass of beer. This was my way to be his friend so that he would be confident enough to teach me the art of baking. The 'maestro' trusted me. He said, 'Whatever I tell you in terms of the mixture, remember it well. But I teach you and you alone. I do not want that what I taught you is learned by others. I trust that later on you will not push me out of my job.' I promised him that I will be faithful. 'If you teach me, I will be grateful. If you give me help, I will also help you.' So, I learned the trade. Every mixture he taught me, I wrote down in a notebook so I would not forget. I filled a notebook with instructions for all kinds of baking. For almost one year I was assistant to the 'maestro'. But there was also a hazard in baking. One could cut one's fingers by accident with the rollers. At night, when work stopped, I would study the oven. It was big. I was fascinated when holding the spade to put in the kneaded dough inside the oven. By the time I learned the art of baking, I had reached a wage of 35 pesos (US$4.38) a month. 'If only I could have a friend to live with, I could study in the evening,' I mused. But I never have been able to study.

I learned that in Pasay, a bakery was looking for a worker. The former worker had stolen funds. When a customer paid his bill, he pocketed the money and left. The boss of this bakery asked me elementary points about baking. I pretended not to know too much, for I would be hired as a helper. 'Roger, do you know how to mix dough for bread?' 'If it is only ordinary bread, I could easily learn it.' I told him, 'You can mix the ingredients, I will put every mixture inside the oven.' But I showed my boss what I knew. He was surprised the next day that there were many kinds of bread for sale.

I stayed in this bakery for three years. A girl entered work. She was a widow. I thought she was beautiful. I courted her only in jest. My boss, however, was not giving me my pay. Sometimes I would ask for the amount due me. I would ask for US$6.50; I would be given only $2.50. I would ask for 100 pesos (US$12.50); I would be given only $4.50. What a life that was. All I needed — soap, Colgate, toothbrush, coffee, sugar — I had to borrow from the store. Pretty soon my debts were increasing. They reached 1,075 pesos (US$134.37), but where is the money I earned? So, I asked the beautiful widow to live with me. 'Let's elope. This is no life here. We can never make progress in this job,' I told her. And the girl willingly left with me. We were holding on to our 75 pesos (US$9.37). We reached Bulacan (a province close to Manila). I left her with a friend and then returned to Manila where I started again from scratch. My wage was 90 pesos (US$11.25) a month. But my boss was strict. He did not like me to visit Bulacan. I quarrelled with a worker. He was from another province . . . a drunkard. He boxed me; I kicked him back and he fell on the floor. He broke a glass case. So I hurriedly left, afraid I had to pay for the damage. Back in Bulacan, I tried working in a quarry. One truck of stones would give me 12 pesos (US$1.50). I saved 70 pesos (US$8.75) from this job. I returned to Manila and trained as a bus conductor for a busline called Cometa Liner. But I lost all my savings during training. I spent much trying to get a driver's licence. In the end I had only 85 centavos (US$0.11).

I heard of a friend who was working in a bakery in Pasig. I decided to find him. If I couldn't see him, I would go back to Bulacan and do the job in the quarry once again. I walked from Guadalupe to Pasig (a distance of about 15 km). I was taken in. This time the name of the bakery was New Year Bakery. While I was taken in as a simple helper, my friends were amazed to know that I could do what a 'maestro' could do. My salary was raised from 45 pesos (US$5.62) to 120 pesos (US$15) a month. I was overjoyed. I wanted to return to my wife, whom I had not seen for quite some time. I thought I could bring her to Pasig with the money I earned. I felt good having a job and knowing she also had one. But to my greatest surprise, I soon learned that she had another husband. Worse, she left with all my clothes. What a mishap, nothing was left to me. I felt very bad. I cried not for her but for my clothes. Unfortunately, I couldn't stay long in the job. My boss was the type of man who when he was angry would scold us all. I couldn't stand it. I told my boss I couldn't cope with the work and I left.

My auntie knew of a massage clinic on 4th Avenue. I was asked to look for girls for the clinic. You know how men are. They like to go on outings. So I asked the boss for an allowance so I could look for girls. I courted one girl and got her in. I was able to recruit 12 girls. For each girl that I recruited I earned one peso. I wasn't happy with the money I earned. I thought I was doing something wrong. I used to walk and walk. Once, I reached the place of my first boss.

My former boss was happy to see me and invited me to work with him again. He still did not know that I could be a 'maestro' in a bakery. He took me in for US$11.25 a month. He promised me that he would increase my salary the moment the bakery was earning a bit more. The 'maestro' in the bakery was a stout person who loved to sleep. What I did to display my skills was to do the work while he was asleep. My Chinese boss saw it all and was pleased. He bought some more baking equipment and the bakery progressed. But I got tired of the job.

It was at that time that I came to know my present wife. I forgot to tell you that I once lived with a lady from Batangas (a provincial town). You know how men are. I am fond of girls, but usually girls would reject me. With my wife in Batangas, I had a child. She also left me. The child remained with me. It is the lady who was willing to care for my child who is now my present wife.

I soon left the bakery due to a conflict with the boss who accused me of stealing bread. I felt very much hurt. God knows I did not cheat my boss. Afraid that I would kill in my anger, I left the bakery. My wife was working as a helper for someone dealing with spare parts of airplanes. As I did not have a job, my wife's boss invited me to do some work, cleaning spare parts of airplanes. He said I could stay in the house, eat in his house and work on the spare parts. When there is no work I could even sleep there. But he did not talk to me about money. Since he was quite good, I accepted the offer. By God's mercy, whenever he earned 10,000 pesos (US$1,250) or 20,000 pesos (US$2,500), he would give an amount to each one of us. In that sense, he was good.

My wife gave birth to our eldest child. With the birth of a baby, I have become a real family man. I thought it was time again to look for another job. I went to Novaliches to a cousin of mine. I became a construction worker with a wage of 12 pesos (US$1.50) a day. Then I tried to save for things for the house. I would buy spoons, plates, etc., sometimes on credit. When I had acquired some household goods, I tried to work as a mason. I was accepted with a daily wage of 18 pesos (US$2.25). My wage increased. I was able to rent a house at 80 pesos (US$10) a month. There were times I couldn't pay the rent. There were times we had to borrow money for our food . . . until we were driven out of the house. I felt exploited. We housed ourselves in another squatter area. A bit later, all houses were demolished by the authorities. I was asked to go to the resettlement area in Sapang Palay. The demolition team of the authorities failed to take us to the resettlement site. By God's mercy I was able to find another house. But I could hardly afford the rent. My wage was not sufficient. I found another construction job. Sometimes I had to borrow money for transportation.

One time I told myself, 'When I get my thirteenth month pay, I shall buy cigarettes with it.' This was the start of my work as a cigarette vendor. With US$8.75, I was able to buy a pack of Hope, a half pack of Philip Morris, a half pack of Marlboro and 50 pieces of Storck candy. By God's mercy I was able to earn more. Every afternoon, I would sell cigarettes. At midnight, I would sleep. In the morning, I would go on this job. I had wanted to look for a fixed place from which to sell. But I was always being driven out. What I can say about cigarette vending is that you never have a fixed place. I went to so many busy streets. I was always driven out. Finally I landed in the National Food Authority (NFA) building. The security guard of the building did not like me. But I was always coming back and being driven out again. Later I got to know the caretaker (a woman) of the building. I pleaded with her to let me stay. I promised her to keep the place clean. I told her it was my only means of livelihood. I even lied by saying that I was in prison before. 'If only I could buy a half ganta of rice daily and some dried fish,

I would be happy. I would rather do this than steal,' I told her. The caretaker took pity on me. For a number of years now I am selling cigarettes in front of the NFA building.

I must say I have tried to be good to our neighbours. Through cigarette vending, I was able to buy a bicycle, a tricycle, furniture for the house . . . we eat three times a day. This has been my story . . . how I became a cigarette vendor.

Cigarette Vendor 10: Why doesn't the government give the cigarette vendors a fixed place to sell? We can contribute to the government. Why not? Everyday they can collect 2 pesos from each one of us. And in Metro-Manila, I estimate that there are at least 1 million vendors. This means that the government can collect 2 million pesos (US$108,108). Instead of arresting us and paying $5.40 bail money, which doesn't go to the government anyway, the government should be giving us a real opportunity to earn.

Notes

1. E.F. Schumacher, *Small is Beautiful*. London: Cox and Wyman, 1973.

2. Peter L. Berger, 'Putting Sociology in Place', in R.M. Kloss, R.E. Roberts and D.S. Dorn (eds), *Sociology With A Human Face*. Saint Louis: C.V. Mosby, 1976. According to Berger, 'humanistic psychologists try to analyze the motivations of self-actualizing individuals, while humanistic sociologists attempt to analyze human institutions critically . . . to see if they frustrate or enhance human potentials' (pp. 1–15).

3. Aloysius Pieres, 'Towards a Liberating Asian Theology and Spirituality', *Makatao*, 1983, 3(1, 2):43–51. Manila: Asian Social Institute.

4. Third General Conference of the Latin American Bishops, *Puebla: Evangelization at Present and in the Future of Latin America*. Middlegreen: St Paul Publications, 1980. This document describes the situation of injustice as 'the deep-rooted social differences, the extreme poverty and the violation of human rights' (no. 90). It also refers to 'structures that have proved to be well-springs of injustice . . . linked with the expansion of liberal capitalism . . . and arising out of ideologies of the dominant culture' (no. 473).

5. *ibid*. A situation of social sinfulness refers to the 'growing gap between rich and poor as a scandal and a contradiction of Christian existence . . . a situation contrary to the plan of the Creator and to the honour that is due Him' (no. 28). See also L. Boff and X. Clodovis, *Salvation and Liberation: In Search of a Balance Between Faith and Politics*. Quezon City: Claretian Fathers, 1985.

6. A team from a religious congregation in the USA analysed itself and came out with the following indictment: 'If we are honest, we must admit that much of the religion preached on the networks and in some schools and parishes is pious hucksterism, and exploitation of religious yearnings in the name of financial achievements, feathered clerical and ministerial nests and the husbandry of powers. The question we must face squarely is the domestication of our faith. In seeking the patronage of the culture and the people of power, we must ask ourselves whether a terrible intimidation of belief has occurred. Has the Faith been overcome?' (*INFO on Human Development*, (Manila), 8(9):9, Office for Human Development of the Federation of Asian Bishops.

7. Willy Brandt, *Common Crisis: North–South Cooperation for World Recovery*, the Brandt Commission 1983. London and Sydney: Pan Books, 1983. See also Renato Constantino, *The Nationalist Alternative*. Quezon City: Foundation for Nationalist Studies, 1979.

8. Virginia Unsworth, *Trilateralism*. Development and Asia Series no. 5.

Hongkong: Centre for the Progress of Peoples, 1980. See also: Constantino, op. cit., p. 6.

9. 'Export Processing Zones in Asia', APHD Newsletter, no. 11, 1981 (based on a preliminary research undertaken on behalf of APHD by Dennis Shoesmith, Asian Bureau, Australia); 'Tourism in Asia', APHD Newsletter, no. 10, 1981. See also: Constantino, op. cit., pp. 28, 30–1, 34–6, 43, 49.

10. Jose Comblin, *The Church and the National Security State*. New York: Orbis Books, 1979.

11. An analysis of the World Information and Communication Order is contained in *Many Voices, One World*. New York: UNESCO, 1980.

12. Brendan Lovatt, 'Faith and Politics' (edited by Sr. Pauline McAndrew), unpublished manuscript, 1985.

13. Mina Ramirez and Gerard Rikken, 'Participatory Research in the Field of Communication', *Makatao*, 1984, 4(1, 2):35. The signs of hope referred to are those which are cited in the article. These are:

— In the field of politics, there are ongoing organizing activities among groups of farmers, fishermen, cultural minorities, women, teachers and so on to contribute as groups to the building of a more just and humane society, and also to protest about basic social issues.

— In the field of economics, the move is towards appropriate technology and cooperatives.

— In the field of education, the stress is on non-formal education.

— In the field of health, the emphasis is on paramedical programmes and community-based health care.

— In the field of family education, the role of the family in the community is underscored.

— In the field of media, micro-media and group media become an alternative to counteract the adverse effects of mass media (which through advertisements promote consumerism);

— In the field of religion, basic Christian communities or 'Christians in basic human communities' (in the case of non-Christian Asia) are important. In these small groupings, religion embraces the whole of life's realities — political, economic, social, cultural and so on. Authentic expression of the faith has particular, if not essential, relevance to issues of justice, freedom and peace.

In the Philippines, there are four institutions which are Asian in the scope of their operation for the development of alternative media: Asian Social Institute (ASI), Communication Foundation for Asia (CFA), Philippine Educational Theatre Association (PETA), and Sonolux Asia.

14. Sr. Mary John Mananzan, 'The Filipino Woman Before and After the Spanish Conquest in the Philippines', unpublished research material, 1985.

15. Renato Constantino, *Identity and Consciousness: The Philippine Experience*. Manila: Malaya Books. Constantino gives an incisive account of the 'legacy of ignorance' handed to the Filipinos by the colonial power. During the Spanish rule, 'intellectual curiosity, a tendency to think for oneself, was viewed with suspicion and discouraged. The people learned that it was safer not to question and became accustomed to leave the thinking to their social superiors. Thus when an indigenous elite developed, they too were conceded by the masses the right to think for them.' On the other hand, 'the elite, though they were eventually accorded the privileges of education and Hispanic culture and therefore gained from inputs of information and

had vistas of a wider world, still suffered from a thinking that was circumscribed by the values of the colonizer. . . . they saw reality in terms of their Hispanized upbringing . . . and looked at their society and people through the prism of colonial culture. . . . And yet, like the masses, they retained a feeling of inferiority, in their case because they were not wholly Hispanized. . . . While they claimed to be the spokesmen of the people, they were to a large extent already alienated from them as they were also alienated from Hispanization. This ambivalence was to survive through various epochs.'

16. Patrick Williams and Joan Thornton Pearce, *The Vital Network*. London: Greenwood Press, 1979.

17. In most Third World cities, one of the phenomena that may strike a Westerner is the countless number of people who practically stay in the streets to eke out an existence. This is true of Manila, with its population of about 8 million people.

18. The cigarette vendors in the streets of Manila are of two types: (1) the vendor who has a fixed place by the sidewalk; and (2) the mobile vendor who runs between buses, cars and small vehicles called 'jeepneys' to sell one or more cigarettes or candy to drivers and passengers. Lighting the cigarette of a customer is an extra service rendered by the vendor.

19. A 'maestro' in a bakery is the term used to refer to the master-baker who is in charge of mixing the ingredients for baking. The 'maestro' is supposed to keep the recipes of special bakery products secret.

8

Alternative communication for women's movements in Latin America

Moema Viezzer

The United Nations 'Conference for Women', held in Nairobi, Kenya, in July 1985, powerfully demonstrated the important role played by communication media in the international women's movement. The fact that over 250 films dealing with women's issues were presented at this major international forum showed that film is a strong and effective medium for conveying reality.

In the case of national and international systems of mass media, however, the situation is different. In Latin America, for example, those who directly suffer the consequences of the misuse of radio, television, film and the press, know that they are objects of oppression for people and institutions who hold economic and political power. As far as women are concerned, these media are channels of male domination which systematically reinforce oppression on a worldwide scale.

In the face of this we have seen — especially over the last ten years — an increasing determination among women in general, and among a small percentage of men, to bring about change. Initiatives have taken various forms and range from a sustained attempt to discredit the image of women portrayed by the mass media to finding new ways of using traditional media, and even inventing new methods of communication. Some of these initiatives are described in the following pages, which deal mainly with alternative communication and grassroots education among women in Latin America.

Changing the image of women

In the 1970s a movement began to change the traditional image of women in the media. The United Nations' Women's Decade has helped to lift the debate on to an international level, creating a surge of interest in women's issues. However, the mass media in general still portray a traditional view of woman, limiting her to her 'privileged' position — domestic life — in which her prime role is to serve the world of men.

The new territories that have been won in the media for women are still very limited, and although there are possibilities for further change, these are not likely to affect the social structure. The mass media provide no real opportunity for the discussion of women's concerns, nor do they serve as a serious means of communication between women. On the other hand, there has been an increase in the use of alternative methods of communication, developed specifically for women mainly by feminist groups. In Brazil, for example, the newspapers *Nos Mulheres* (We Women), *Brasil Mulher* (Brazilian Woman) and *Mulherio* (Little Woman) serve a committed readership, and some headway has been made by women in radio and television. Throughout the Latin American continent ILET (Instituto Latinoamericano de Estudios Transnacionales) is doing important work, and ISIS (Women's International Information and Communication Service) is one of the most comprehensive women's networks in the world. Both organizations produce alternative publications and documentation, which are of good quality but have only a small circulation, mainly within the groups that help to produce them. These important initiatives are restricted by problems such as illiteracy — in the case of the press — and the high cost of other media, such as film and video.

One trend that is becoming increasingly important in the women's movement is the growth of communication systems among the poorer sectors of society. These alternative methods of communication serve the interests of the women's struggle against oppression throughout Latin America. In particular, they help women to reflect and act on issues related to the subordination of women by men and to the struggle for more equal conditions in society. There is no doubt that, out of this movement, a new female psychology is emerging. The problem is to find effective ways to communicate this new movement and its vision — the 'new woman'.

The communication opportunities open to the grassroot women's movement do not compare with the importance of the large numbers of women's groups among the poorer sections of society that have sprung up as a result of civil rights campaigns. In Brazil, an estimated 80 percent of the protest movements are made up of women. Women, who constitute over half the population of the Latin American countries, play an important role in the social and economic structures of our nations. Despite this latent power, the various attempts at consolidating the women's movement through initiatives such as film collectives, alternative newspapers, audiovisual materials, magazines and newsletters are largely isolated efforts, which fail to make an impact either in individual countries or in Latin America as a whole.

There is still an enormous need throughout the continent for genuine communication between women from the poorer classes. It has become apparent that, although past initiatives have involved poorer groups, women from the middle classes who promote and direct the work, publishing the results and then planning future efforts, have actually benefited most. These are women who enjoy a very different level of income, education and situation in society. Their concerns and attitudes are often at odds with the very women they seek to serve.

It must be said that these initiatives have added considerably to the analysis and momentum of the women's movement, but at the same time they have not been controlled by the groups they represent — the majority of women in Latin American societies. While it is true that many grassroot groups and movements seek to promote greater participation and integration for women in the social development of a country, the methods that are employed often tend to maintain — and sometimes reinforce — the dependence and oppression of women in the poorer sectors.

In the first place, the emancipation of women presupposes the elimination of the underlying injustice of exploitation — of both men and women. More equal distribution of wealth and power will only come about with the dismantling of class differences. But we need to go beyond that: to try and release women from their place of subordination to men — an ancient and universal phenomenon which persists even in countries with socialist systems of government, and which stands as a barrier to all human progress. A final point to remember is that female liberation also entails eliminating forms of oppression among women themselves. In the same way that divisions of class, race and religion pervade the whole of society, so too can women's submission to men be found at all levels of society.

In this context there is a need to find appropriate methods of research, action and communication which will take into account the different and complex situations of oppression that characterize the lives of most Latin American women. It is certain that only initiatives *by* women, *for* women, *among* women will consolidate the women's movement as part of the wider grassroot movement.

Alternative systems of communication among women

Without making any further comments on the situation of women in Latin America, I would like to mention a number of organizations in Latin America that express, in different ways, the 'new style' of woman that is emerging on that continent. Their methods range from person-to-person or group work to the setting up of entire networks of communication.

Rede Mulher (Women's Network) — Brazil

The broad objective of Rede Mulher is to liaise between women's groups and organizations with the aim of promoting more harmony and justice in society as a whole, and particularly in male–female relationships.

Rede Mulher works for the grassroot women's movement at a local, national and international level. It helps women's groups and organizations to gain a deeper understanding of the problems they face and to look for the right solutions. It also liaises with other women's groups around the world.

Grassroot communication among women is the basis for Rede Mulher's activities, including an analysis of a particular group's situation by means of participatory surveys and a continual process of education. The work is carried out among the most oppressed sectors of society: housewives in the poor districts, women in domestic service, workers in industry and the service sector and others. In the same way as it builds up support networks among these groups, Rede Mulher seeks to create similar networks among women of other social sectors who are committed to the struggle for the liberation of women. Currently, or recently, Rede Mulher has been involved in the following activities.

One project in São Paulo, Brazil, sought to trace the history of the mothers' and women's groups in the region. Some 154 representatives of the groups contributed to a study of their aims, the way in which they are organized, and their relation to institutions like the Church, the State, political parties and other women's groups. The survey lasted from November 1983 to June 1985.

The project got underway with an analysis of all the material that had previously been published on the subject, and the eastern and southern districts of São Paulo were chosen as the areas of study. The city of São Paulo is Brazil's largest, with 10 million inhabitants, and is the centre of the metropolitan region made up of 37 townships known as Greater São Paulo. It is the nation's most powerful industrial and financial centre, producing 25 percent of the national income. The city has serious social problems. Some 4 million people live in inadequate housing, and many of the communities on the outskirts of the city lack basic services.

These social and economic problems have made São Paulo a centre for workers' organizations and other social movements. The mothers' clubs and women's groups in the outlying slum districts are gaining momentum and today there are over 2,000, attended by some 15,000 women who meet together every week or two in groups of between 10 and 30. Some of these clubs and groups have taken an active part in broader social movements, such as the Cost of Living Campaign and pressure groups demanding water and sewage services and other basic necessities. More recently, they played an influential role in the campaign for direct elections and for measures against unemployment.

The participatory survey coordinated by Rede Mulher has enabled the clubs and groups to reconstruct their own history and to compile a list of 94 clubs in the eastern district alone. The communication process sparked off by the survey bears a number of different features. Several regional meetings were held to discuss the survey and to analyse the results. There has been a marked increase in visits between clubs within the regions. There have been more organized activities between women from different regions, especially as a result of the committees that were created to draw up the results of the survey.

The survey showed five different forms of participatory communication, which are now being used to convey the information back to the groups themselves. A manual has been produced giving a step-by-step account of the survey, with the educational and communication processes that were involved — all in clear and simple terms. There is also a booklet giving statistical details of the survey, with a description and location of the 94 clubs and groups in the eastern district. Interviews with some of the women who took part have been worked into a play called 'For Being a Woman'. It deals with the problems they face as they try to organize themselves and find solutions. An audio visual programme, 'What Now, Maria? . . . ', shows the daily lives of women in their homes and in the groups. Finally, the history of the clubs and groups is depicted in a magazine which was co-produced with the grassroot education group of São Paulo's Catholic University.

In addition to the resources that have sprung from the São Paulo survey, Rede Mulher has done pioneering work in compiling a library of slide presentations and video cassettes which are loaned to discussion groups, meetings and workshops. Tentative forays have also been made into the mass media. For the first time, a series of ten interviews has been broadcast on the programme 'TV Woman' of Globo Televisaõ, the largest in Brazil. Ten women who took part in the survey of mothers' clubs were asked to share their opinions on a whole range of topics such as health, sexuality, children's education and party politics. This was an important opportunity to reach the 15 million viewers throughout the country who normally watch this programme. There are plans for a programme on women to be broadcast in 1986 by University Radio of São Paulo. It will be recorded in the areas where the women live, rather than in the studios.

In all its projects, Rede Mulher stresses that the production and use of different methods of communication are not an end in themselves, but serve the grassroot women's movement.[1]

Latin American Network for Women's Education — CEAAL
This network is part of the programme of the Consejo de Educacion
de Adultos de America Latina. CEAAL (the Council for Adult
Education in Latin America) works in cooperation with national
organizations and also by developing specific programmes in
different subject areas. The network was first coordinated from
Venezuela by Rosa Paredes, but its roots go back to 1980. In that year
the Canada-based International Council for Adult Education
(ICAE) included the subject of women's participation in its research
work on adult education.

The first stage of that research consisted of surveys in seven regions
of the Third World: Africa, the Arab countries, the Caribbean,
South Asia, South-east Asia, Latin America and the South Pacific.
It culminated in a conference in Udaipur, India, where participants
shared the results of the surveys. In preparation for the conference,
a Latin American workshop on grassroot women's projects was
organized in Caracas, Venezuela, in November 1981. Since then,
women working in grassroot education programmes throughout
the South American continent have kept in regular contact with
each other. In September 1983 a second Latin American workshop expanded on the issues that were raised in 1981. The participants also agreed to set up a Latin American Team for Women's
Projects, with the continent divided into the following regions:
Southern Cone, Andean countries, Brazil, Mexico and Central
America.

The team started off with three projects: a quarterly newsletter,
which maintains contact with individuals and group members of the
network; a continent-wide project of study and action on adult
education and women's organizations; and a series of workshops on
the methodology of grassroots education for women. These
workshops provided the first opportunity for exchange between the
regions, and their final evaluation took place in November 1985
during the World Assembly for Adult Education held in Buenos
Aires, Argentina.

The programme of workshops enabled each meeting to be part
of a process rather that just an 'event'. The results of the workshops will be redistributed among women's groups in the various
countries. It is a process that enables the participants to move
from specific to general issues and then return to the specific with
a broader vision and a deeper understanding of how grassroot
education can be a powerful instrument of support to the women's
movement.[2]

ISIS International
Established in 1984, Isis International is an information and communication service for women. It is run by a group of women whose purpose is to help in the exchange of ideas, experiences and information and to offer contacts among groups and individuals interested in women's concerns throughout the world. The Isis headquarters is in Rome, with an office in Santiago de Chile.[3]

The organization has various functions which include: encouraging dialogue between women around the world; strengthening national, regional and international women's networks; and providing information and guidance to groups of women who are working to combat female oppression. It works through a network of over 10,000 contacts in 150 countries, and its documentation centre receives thousands of magazines, newsletters and studies from all parts of the world. The subject matter is broad — health, alternative communication, development, peace — in fact, any areas in which women are involved.

Among its many services, Isis produces an international women's magazine which provides a forum for groups that are active in the women's movement. Each edition is compiled with the help of one or more groups from Third World countries. Another publication is *Women in Action*, which is a supplement to the magazine and gives news and information on groups, events, conferences and courses. Both are published twice a year in English and Spanish. Isis has also organized international meetings on women's communication which bring together participants from different countries with experience in the use of alternative methods of communication.

In the arena of international law, Isis was one of the founder members of Feminist Network, formed in the International Tribunal on Crimes against Women, in March 1976 in Belgium. The purpose of the network is to stimulate international support for women who have suffered violation of their rights. The network is also used to convey up-to-date information on campaigns and particular events organized by women (for which Isis relies on contacts working for the network in some 30 countries).

Another international organization formed by Isis is the Women's Health Network for Latin America and the Caribbean. This has been operating since 1984 in Santiago de Chile, disseminating information and materials on women's health groups. In a monthly newsletter it covers subjects such as occupational health, sexuality, birth control, natural or alternative medicine, population control and mental health.

During the 1985 UN Conference for Women in Nairobi, Isis International was one of the organizers of a workshop on women and the communication media. The discussion was divided into three broad groups: Asia, Africa and Latin America. In the Latin American group there was general agreement that considerable resources already exist, produced for women by women, in the form of videos, slides, radio programmes and alternative newspapers. Nevertheless, there were two suggestions which would improve existing work. One was to find a way to share resources between groups in different countries, perhaps by creating a travelling media library for use throughout the continent. A Latin American network for communication media for women is being formed for that purpose, and to serve as a centre of information. The other suggestion was to explore more deeply the concept of alternative communication for women by organizing seminars on the content, language and methods of the media available in Latin America.

Strengthen and consolidate media work
This glimpse of three of the communication networks serving women in Latin America and the Caribbean demonstrates the concern and commitment of the large numbers of women who long to see the authoritarian society of Latin America transformed. Over the past few years, despite considerable political and financial obstacles, women have learnt to express themselves and their messages through numerous forms and methods. Wall charts, games, cartoons, newsletters, drama and music groups, film and video — these are just a few examples of the media they use.

These media can truly be called alternative, not only because they are developed by women at grassroots level, but also because they are produced according to different criteria, in contrast to the 'packages' that are prepared for the mass media. They are produced and used by groups of women who are committed to social change. The challenge facing the women's networks in Latin America is to consolidate and strengthen their media work in order to make inroads into the vast commercial interests of the mass media. Their most difficult task is to be heard and seen in the public arena.

The communication media are powerful instruments that influence both the opinion and the values of the public. Alternative communication — above all grassroots communication — is helping to create a new cultural outlet serving the women's movement. In many cases, participatory communication has become an integral part of the women's movement, and therefore part of an educational process which is forming the 'new image' and the 'new woman' who, in her turn, creates the 'new society'.

Notes

1. Rede Mulher: Caixa Postal 1803, 01051 São Paulo, SP, Brazil.
2. Council for Adult Education in Latin America (CEAAL): Casilla 6257, Santiago 22, Chile.
3. Isis International: (a) via Santa Maria dell'Anima 30, 00186 Rome, Italy; (b) Casilla 2067, Correo Central, Santiago, Chile.

9

Communication and religion in the technological era

William F. Fore

For years I have heard church leaders and church communicators pose a question that usually takes more or less the same form. We are in the midst of changes in communication, they say, and these changes are so profound that we appear to be entering a new age — the Age of Information. But the churches seem to be largely unaware of these changes, or even to be resisting them. How can we get the churches to take these changes seriously? How can we get the churches to become really involved in radio, television, satellite and computers? That is, how can we get religion to join the communication revolution?

This seems to be a fairly straightforward challenge to the churches to become more relevant to the times in which we live. But the argument contains so many questionable assumptions, and states the problem so perversely, that it can lead religious communication planning and action dangerously astray; indeed, it has already done so.

I propose here to try to reveal the partly mistaken assumptions and observations behind this argument, and to suggest an alternative view as to what is the appropriate role of the Christian church in facing the challenges of the new communication technologies.

My points are three: first, that the Age of Information is in fact a symptom of a larger, more significant, change, namely, a worldwide shift to the Technological Era; second, that the church has already taken this shift seriously but has responded primarily by either rejection or accommodation; and third, that a more appropriate stance for the church is a different alternative, namely, creative transformation.

The Technological Era
That we are in the midst of fundamental change there can be little doubt. In many respects these changes are bringing about a new kind of world. Robert Oppenheimer, the nuclear scientist who supervised development of the first successful atomic device, saw the change this way:

This world of ours is a new world, in which the unity of knowledge,the nature of human communities, the order of society, the order of ideas, the very notions of society and culture have changed and will not return to what they have been in the past.[1]

This is my first point: *that the religions of the world are facing not just a new Age of Information but a new Technological Era, which brings with it an alternative worldview that challenges the worldviews of all the historical religions.*

The challenge comes not merely from more efficient, pervasive and persuasive means of communication, not only from a whole new cluster of technologies that extend the eyes and ears and knowledge and power and control of humans farther and faster than ever before. While it is true to say that we are entering an Age of Information, this is not nearly the whole truth. Behind the electronics and the techniques there is emerging a whole new worldview, which itself challenges every one of the historical religions, and which can lead either to humankind's next integrative steps towards new religious insights and meaning, or to the collapse of religious consciousness and the emergence of a period of anarchy and despair.

It is not enough to call what we are experiencing 'rapid social change' or even 'revolution', since these connote only social or political upheaval. The change is more basic, in that it modifies everything we have known before. Arend van Leewen suggests that there have been only two basic eras in all of history.[2] The first is the ontocratic era, in which we have lived until now. Always before, human society has apprehended life as a cosmic totality, where belief in a god or gods outside human experience held together the contradictory and confusing elements of the human community. But relatively suddenly,within the last 300 years, we have moved away from this unifying concept into a multiform system of relationships, with no specific cornerstone, no single integrating element that gives all other things their reason for being. We have moved into the Technological Era, and this is the great new fact of our time. The communication revolution, the Age of Information, the Information Society — these are surface manifestations of the more profound change that is under way in every aspect of life.

The Technological Era is functional and pragmatic, characterized by utilitarianism and relativism. It is supported by three philosophical views. The first is rationality, the idea that meaningful lives must be amenable to reason. The second is autonomy, which holds that people can find in themselves and their world the norms and goals for their own existence. The third is humanism, which asserts that this space–time world is the proper home for humankind, rejects metaphysical claims ('they will be rewarded in Heaven'), and demands that religion deal with the here-and-now.

Taken together, these three views describe secularization. But this understanding of secularization is not necessarily inconsistent with the Christian faith. The proclamation of the Gospel is precisely that God acts in history, that the eternal order is revealed in the historical order. The clash with biblical religion comes only when the technological worldview's emphasis upon the pragmatic and the instrumental results in people being treated as means rather than as as ends. It is one thing to deal with the here-and-now; it is quite another to reject the response of faith which insists that ultimate meaning transcends the here-and-now, that meanings are in people, and that, therefore, people are more important than things.

As Jacques Ellul has demonstrated, the new Technological Era has created a world of means, which results in the loss of meaning for human existence.[3] Ellul calls the force at work The Technique, by which he means a style of conduct that pervades our life and governs all of our personal and social activities — a kind of morality. The Technique is essentially a method of problem-solving. It asks, How can we best solve this problem *now*? rather than, What is the ultimate objective and how can we reach it? The means is identified with the end, and whatever gets something 'done' is good.

The communication manifestations of The Technique are literally Orwellian. The Technique's communication does not use fear or threats, nor does it concentrate on undermining its opponent. Rather, it characteristically woos persons, taking their own genuine needs (to be safe, to be liked, to be comfortable) and using them to create other needs which make them not only willing but quite eager to agree to what is being said, to buy what is being sold (the deodorant, the beer, the antacid). As an example, the problem with television news on the commercial TV networks in the USA is that people *prefer* its simplistic presentation over a more complex and demanding one.

This new technological worldview and its communication manifestations are achieving a remarkable unity of acceptance everywhere — not only among the capitalist West and the communist nations, but also in the less technically developed nations. They are aided by the new flows of money, information and power which have followed from the invention of the corporation almost a century ago (which eliminated personal responsibility) and the more recent development of the multinational corporation (which eliminated political and social constraints on economic power).

The new technological worldview poses three specific threats to religion. First, a major portion of the world's interests, motivations, satisfactions and energies is being pulled away from a religious centre

— *any* religious centre. This is symbolized in Europe by the churches having become empty shells, visited only as objects of architectural interest, and in the USA by the growing chasm between what church-goers profess and how they act. Elsewhere in the world, religion functions primarily by its power of taboo and its means of sociali-zation (as in much of Africa), or is used as a device for social or political control (as in India, Iran and elsewhere in the Middle East).

Second, genuine religious vocabularies have lost their power. The symbols, rites, images and references of religion no longer move people. Today most people in the First World relate to — that is, understand, recognize and think about — the images of 'Dallas' and 'Dynasty' far more than they relate to the images of Abraham, Moses and Paul. Biblical images, and most historical Christian images as well, no longer have the power to move, to motivate, to illuminate, to instruct. Rather, they are treated as relics — quaint oddities not to be taken seriously but only to be treated gingerly, as part of a bygone culture.

Third, there is a growth of genuine religious concern which has little or no interest in organized religion. These creative and dynamic religious forces are found not only in film, literature and the arts, but also in some aspects of science and industry, where thoughtful people are seeking ways to give institutional expression to their basic religious concerns while at the same time rejecting alliances with institutional religion. Alcoholics Anonymous, drug rehabilitation centres, coalitions for social and political reforms, therapy clusters, the adult education movement: these and other activities provide opportunities for people to 'get involved' — without the benefit of clergy. We are seeing de-Christianized activities emerge in Western culture — a growing expression of religious faith which rejects the traditional organizational expressions of that faith.

The new media environment
Each of these three dangers to organized religion is manifested clearly and powerfully in the mass media. For it is through the media that the alternative worldview is taught, unintended perhaps, but nevertheless with great persuasiveness and power. Alternatives to traditional religious values are made tremendously appealing. The religious vocabulary is supplanted by a vocabulary comprised of a curious mix of economics, science, high technology and fantasy. Good examples of this new vocabulary are found in the films of George Lucas (*Star Wars*), Stanley Kubric (*2001*) and Stephen Spielberg (*Close Encounters of The Third Kind* and *E.T.*) At the same time, activities of persons with genuine religious motivation are

secularized, glamorized and finally robbed of their religious rootage. Even Martin Luther King and Mother Teresa have not been strong enough religious images to completely escape this commercialization and secularization.

Although we have lived within the new media environment for only a few decades, some of its characteristics are becoming clear:

1. an increasing dependence on mediated communication as distinct from face-to-face communication; more time spent with electronics, less spent with people;

2. an increasing number of communication delivery systems, together with a greater diversification of programming, so that individuals can pick and choose only those messages which reinforce *already held* attitudes and beliefs. This results in cultural fragmentation whereby people literally cannot hear or see others;

3. a shift from treating communication as a service function essential to the welfare of the whole society (like water and roads) to treating it as a commodity to be purchased and sold; and, as media structures are increasingly controlled by the laws of economics, they inevitably become larger and controlled by fewer people;

4. a trivialization of all news, information and entertainment for the vast majority of people, where emphasis is given to knowledge rather than meaning, surface events rather than depth and reflection, while at the same time sophisticated communication facilities are available to a small elite for their personal growth, education and enrichment, through computer programs, data bases, specialized video cassettes and a wide assortment of information services. This results in a new two-class society — the information-rich and the information-poor.

As the new worldview permeates cultures worldwide, the mass media are increasingly coopted as a tool of the production–consumption cycle rather than as a source of the education, information and entertainment essential to the well-being of citizens. First in the USA, but now more and more in Europe, Japan and elsewhere, radio and television are used essentially for only one thing: to deliver an audience to an advertiser (or a government). Listeners and viewers are being increasingly treated as commodities rather than as persons. As this trend becomes more pronounced, the information which is necessary for citizens to make the kind of informed decisions which could reverse the trend is itself becoming increasingly scarce, until eventually the mass media may provide only circuses for the masses, who embrace it gladly and no longer can tell what they are missing.

Of course, the values and assumptions of this commercialized and secularized mass media are diametrically opposed to those of all the world's great religions. I have described these media values and assumptions previously:

> Power heads the list: power over others, power over nature. As Hannah Arendt points out, in today's media world it is not so much that power corrupts as that the aura of power, its glamorous trappings, attracts. Close to power are the values of wealth and property, the idea that everything can be purchased and that consumption is an intrinsic good. The values of narcissism, immediate gratification of wants, and creature comforts follow close behind.
>
> Thus the mass media tell us that we are basically good, that happiness is the chief end of life, and that happiness consists in obtaining material goods. The media transform the value of sexuality into sex appeal, the value of self-respect into pride, the value of will-to-live into will-to-power. They exacerbate acquisitiveness into greed; they deal with insecurity by generating more insecurity. They change the value of recreation into competition and the value of rest into escape. And perhaps worst of all, the media constrict our experience and substitute media world for real world so that we are becoming less and less able to make the fine judgments that a complex world requires.[4]

Paul Tillich had a term for that which stands at the very opposite of Christian grace and love.[5] He called it 'the demonic'. The demonic is not mere negation; rather, it is found in the combination of genuine creative power together with perversion of Christian values. The demonic affirms that which is less than God and pretends it is God — money, power, prestige. It operates in the individual's wilful yielding to the temptation to give rein to the libido of sensuality, of power and of knowledge, and it operates even more powerfully in human institutions than in individuals.

The power and perversion of commercial television, especially in the USA today, can be said to be demonic. Scarcely any better description could be given to it than that provided by Tillich in 1948, long before television arrived on the scene. During the past thirty years commercial television has become a powerful embodiment of form-creating and form-destroying energy in our lives, an embodiment of the demonic.

Rejection and accommodation

This brings us to the second point: that *church leadership has in fact been aware of both the fundamental shift to the Technological Era and the new information techniques which communicate its worldview, but their responses have been largely inadequate.* They recognize that there has occurred a major shift in values and assumptions, and they have responded in ways that reflect the historical responses which religion has always given to the challenges of opposing worldviews.

After all, this situation is nothing new to the Christian church. Christians *always* find themselves at odds with the values and assumptions found in secular society. Today the problem may be different in degree, if van Leewen is correct. But Christians have always faced the problem of how to respond to the cultural situation in which they find themselves and which is always more or less antithetical to their faith.

One of the best descriptions of the alternatives open to the church is contained in H. Richard Niebuhr's classic *Christ and Culture*.[6] Niebuhr suggests five typical relationships between the Christian and society, seen both in history and in contemporary life:

1. *Christ against culture*: The monastic orders and sect groups withdraw from society. The requirement of converts is to abandon wholly the customs and institutions of the 'heathen' society. This is exemplified by Puritans of every age. Their favourite biblical quotation is 'Do not love the world or the things in the world' (I John 2:15).

2. *Christ of culture*: There is fundamental agreement between the values of church and society. Jesus is the great hero/teacher who, in concert with democratic principles, works to create a peaceful, cooperative society (Cultural Protestantism).

3. *Christ above culture*: Christianity brings the culture up to a high level of fulfilment; culture leads people to Christ, but Christ enters into the situation from above with gifts which human aspiration cannot attain. There is a constant moving up to higher levels of social attainment — 'drawn up' by Christ (Thomas Aquinas).

4. *Christ and culture in paradox*: This view recognizes the necessity and authority of both Christ and culture, but also their opposition. Life lived in faith is precariously and sinfully in tension between the demands of Christ and of culture, in hope of justification which lies beyond history. From Christ we receive the knowledge and freedom to do what culture teaches or requires us to do (Luther).

5. *Christ the transformer of culture*: Human nature is fallen or perverted, and this perversion is transmitted by the culture; thus Christ stands in judgement to all human institutions. But Christ also converts persons within their culture, through their faith and by turning away from sin and pride (Augustine, Calvin, Wesley).

The religious responses to the challenge of The Technique's communication have varied in ways that fit this Niebuhrian analysis. For example, biblical fundamentalists have tended to reject the appeals of the mass media, and to a certain degree to reject the media themselves. They detect the anti-Christian value system it carries and counsel a return to religious fundamentals which often includes proscriptions against dancing, films, plays and rock concerts; attempts to censor the media, especially films, television and books; and the encouragement of participation in church social events as a substitute for secular cultural offerings. In some instances watching television is prohibited, and in others the faithful are encouraged to watch only 'Christian' networks and programmes. This 'Christ against culture' position recognizes the seriousness of The Technique's appeal and its ability to lure people, especially young people, away from fundamentalism's Puritan values.

The problem is that strong reaction tends to increase the attractiveness of that which is banished. Also the rejection of many cultural experiences tends to leave persons psychologically involuted, intellectually isolated and spiritually subject to the pride and authoritarianism generated by any dogmatic and closed system.

Curiously, other so-called fundamentalists have taken exactly the opposite course: 'Christ of culture'. Having no doubt among themselves about the answers to every religious question, they are led to the conclusion that the most important communication task is to reach others with these answers and to convince them of their validity. They see the success of The Technique in converting people to its value system, and so they apprehend these techniques — especially television, radio and books — to convert people to their own religious views. This 'Christ of culture' response is the impetus behind the Electronic Church, a position which, in the guise of rejecting the values of secular culture, actually embraces them. It also explains why fundamentalist religion has been quick to grasp every new communication technique as it came along — first radio, then shortwave, motion pictures, television, and more recently cable, satellite TV and video cassettes. This is the 'pipeline' theory of communication: when the religious message is reduced to a set of unvarying verbal formulas, the only question is how to build a bigger and better 'pipe' to deliver the message to the recipients.

While the programmes of the 'Christ of culture' approach are rich in the vocabulary of nineteenth-century Christian evangelism, the images, and hence the real messages, resonate with The Technique — the gambits of modern television advertising. But using the techniques of commercial television and radio to achieve the end of Christian communication won't work, as research clearly demonstrates. The people who tune in to the Electronic Evangelists are the already converted and convinced. Thus the Electronic Evangelists are simply using the techniques of the secular world to reinforce views already held by those who are comfortable with an otherworldly, pre-scientific, anthropomorphic God, superimposed on the underlying values of the Technological Era.

But there is another 'Christ of Culture' manifestation in the religious mass media. These are the programmes which appeal to many members of the mainline churches in the USA, people who go to church almost every Sunday yet give little evidence of being uneasy about their deep involvement in secular culture and values. Robert Bellah has shown that most Americans today express a vague religious belief in God, but are utterly incapable of relating their faith to any kind of morally coherent life.[7] 'Feeling good' for them has replaced 'being good', and relationships are based not so much on a religious conviction about the essential worth of every individual as on 'contractual' arrangements, in which each person is considered of value to the extent that he or she is of value to *me*. The question, Is this right or wrong? is replaced by, Is it going to work for me, now? By succumbing to this value system of the technocratic era, while continuing to hold on to the trappings of main-line Christianity, they, too, have adopted a 'Christ of culture' response.

Both secular media and most religious media encourage this cultural religion. In fact, its expressions are perhaps the most pervasive of all the religious responses to The Technique. To be sure, there may be excesses in the media which are too gross for even thoroughly acculturated Christians to ignore — too much sex and violence in films, too many commercials on television, too much acid rain, too many armaments — but these are seen as problems which can be adjusted, reduced and reworked, rather than as expressions of a fundamental dislocation from the centre of their faith. For these nominal Christians, the underlying values of commercial television are in fact *their* values.

Creative transformation
There is a third response of Christians to the challenge of The Technique. This response rejects both the 'Christ against culture' and 'Christ of culture' views. It is hesitant, problematic and ambiguous, but it tries to relate the requirements of historical Christian faith to the current cultural and media reality. It takes very seriously the demonic power within the media, but nevertheless refuses to abandon culture altogether. This response is found primarily among various main-line denominational and interdenominational groups in the USA, and in some of the established churches in Western Europe.

These church groups attempt to relate to the media at two levels. First, they develop programme materials in the media which, in the midst of the secular worldview and its power, try to illumine the human condition, to ask meaningful religious questions, to rediscover religious truths, and even to create a new religious vocabulary which can have meaning and power for the multitudes.

Such a response has very little success in 'worldly' terms, that is, in relation to audience size, income for stations and networks, and the development of national celebrities and media events which can be merchandized — in other words, in terms of all those criteria which normally signify success in the commercial media environment.

At the second level, these groups work within the media industries themselves, and also with the political institutions in the society, to bring about conditions which will allow the media to achieve their considerable potential for good. The objective here is to humanize the structures which govern broadcasting, both by encouraging persons within the industry to 'do well by doing good', and by insisting that the social and economic powers of the industry must be counter balanced by governmental power which expresses politically the concern of citizens for the general public welfare. As in the case with programme production, this media reform approach is not likely to achieve significant success in 'worldly' terms, but the objective from a religious standpoint is nevertheless essential.

This approach tends to fit into the Niebuhrian categories of 'Christ and culture in paradox' and 'Christ transforming culture'. It recognizes the ambiguities and paradoxical nature of the church at work within a system full of powers which potentially corrupt everything they touch, including the church. At the same time, it acts in the belief that testifying to the Good News is a requirement that cannot be avoided, and that, potentially, faith and action based on this liberating gospel do indeed transform structures built upon human sin and pride.

This then is my third point: *that creative transformation of the mass media, both from within and from without, is a necessary objective of the church as it faces the challenges of the Technological Era.*

Christians must reject the utilitarian relativism characteristic of the ethos in which we live, and reassert the radical monotheism of our religious history. We are not at the brink of a religionless future. The quest for meaning is as strong today as it ever was. The problem is that the fundamental questions of meaning are no longer being asked where the people see and hear them — in the mass media of communication. Or, if they are being asked, the questions are not generally recognized for what they are because they are obscured and trivialized by The Technique.

The challenge facing religion today
In the light of this analysis, the challenge to the churches and other religious institutions is three-fold: first, to provide an alternative

environment to the media environment; second, to penetrate the media's environment with images and messages which challenge the media's own values and communicate instead fundamental human values; and third, to teach the faithful how to deal with the mass media without succumbing to their power.

One of the greatest strengths of the church today, particularly in the USA, is the fact of its large and effective infrastructure — the local churches. Churches offer community. There is no other institution in American life today where so many people meet regularly in a face-to-face relationship for anything other than work. This face-to-face environment offers tremendous possibilities for building community in the midst of the pressures to substitute a mediated community, and indeed mediated experience, in the place of face-to-face community. At a time of increasing specialization, the local churches can be the meeting place for a genuine exchange of views, a market-place of ideas and values, a place where, within an environment of Christian love and support, people can deal with controversy in ways that are both reality-oriented and productive.

People have already begun to sense the need to create new forms of community. The growth of special interest hobby groups, the reassertion of town and city street fairs, dances and shopping malls, the increased involvement in citizen action groups — all point to the determination of people to get away from the ersatz world of television and to re-enter the real world. But the church is already in place, and the only question is whether it will do what is required of it. If they respond appropriately, the churches can offer a ready-made environment for rediscovering community. Those who will give direction to the church in the decades immediately ahead need to see this function as a major challenge for institutional religion.

The second task, of penetrating existing media with religious images and vocabulary, requires considerable organization, time and money. For these reasons church relationships with the mass media have tended to operate more at the national level than at the local level. National denominational offices and interdenominational organizations need the understanding and support of local churches and their leaders as they attempt to act as leaven within the loaf of broadcasting and other structures of social communication, to be in the culture but not of it. Much more needs to be done in building local and national citizen action groups to make their presence felt at the governmental level in order to secure media that are responsive to the public interest, both locally and nationally.

The third area of action, media education, is growing in importance. Harvey Cox points out that our main ethical problem is not how to make the choices we see, but how to *see* the choices we have to make. Media education is the process by which individuals are helped to see what the mass media are offering and to understand that we in fact have a choice — to accept or reject that offer. Media education must become a major part of the preparation of children to become adults. It should begin at the earliest levels of school and continue through the entire education process. And adults need special help to catch up with the ways media use and abuse them.

Without mediate citizens, that is, persons who are literate about more than just literature, how can we have meaningful participation of everyone in deciding the way our lives are to be run? How can democracy and an open society exist? How can oligarchies and dictatorships and economic and political tyrannies be overcome?

Only by providing alternative environments to the mass media, using the media for messages about human values and helping viewers to overcome their growing dependence upon the media environment and its values can the church hope to liberate people from control by The Technique, and to set them free from the potential tyranny of the Technological Era.

Notes

1. Robert Oppenheimer, in *Saturday Review of Literature*, 29 June 1963, p. 11.

2. Arend van Leewen, *Christianity in a World History*. Edinburgh: Edinburgh Press, 1964.

3. Jacques Ellul, *The Technological Society*. New York: Alfred A. Knopf, 1967.

4. William F. Fore, 'Mass Media's Mythic World', *Christian Century*, 19 January 1977.

5. Paul Tillich, *The Protestant Era*. Chicago: University of Chicago Press, 1948.

6. Richard Niebuhr, *Christ and Culture*. New York: Harper and Brothers, 1951.

7. Robert Bellah, *Habits of the Heart*, Berkeley: University of California Press, 1985.

Notes on contributors

Paul A. V. Ansah studied at the University of Ghana, at the University of Bordeaux and at the University of London (PhD in French Language and Literature). Later he studied journalism and communication at the University of Wisconsin. He was Senior Lecturer in French 1964–74 and Senior Lecturer in Journalism 1975–79 at the University of Ghana. In 1980 he was appointed director of the School of Journalism and Communication, University of Ghana.

Donna A. Demac is a communications lawyer in New York City and a faculty member of the Interactive Telecommunications Programme at New York University. She is the author of *Keeping America Uninformed: Government Secrecy in the 1980s* (1984) and co-author of *Equity in Orbit: The 1985 ITU Space WARC* (1985). For several years her research has focused on applications regulation of new technologies, and on government information policy.

William F. Fore studied at Yale Divinity School and at Columbia University (PhD in Communication and Education). He was director of visual education for the Methodist Board of Missions 1956–63, and executive director of the Broadcasting and Film Commission for the National Council of the Churches of Christ (NCCC) 1964–72. He is currently Assistant General Secretary for Communications of the NCCC, and President of the World Association for Christian Communication. He is the author of *South Americans All* (1960), *Communication for Churchmen* (1968), and *How Man Comes Through in the Mass Media* (1970).

James D. Halloran (DSc) studied at the University of Hull, and at the University of Tampere, Finland. He is currently Director of the Centre for Mass Communication Research, University of Leicester, and President of the International Association for Mass Communication Research. He is the author of *Control or Consent* (1963), *Attitude Formation and Change* (1967), *Demonstrations and Communication: A Case Study* (1970), *The Effects of Mass Communication* (1971), and *Understanding Television: Research and the Broadcaster* (1977).

Cees J. Hamelink is Professor of International Communication at the Institute of Social Studies, The Hague, Netherlands. He received his doctorate from the University of Amsterdam and has lectured on various aspects of international communications in Mexico, the USSR, the USA, Switzerland, India, Hong Kong, Belgium and France. He is the author of *Cultural Autonomy in Global Communications* (1983).

Seán MacBride, SC, Irish barrister and politician, was Irish Minister for External Affairs 1948–51, Secretary-General of the International Commission of Jurists 1963–71, and Chairman of Amnesty International 1961–74. He was awarded the Nobel Peace Prize in 1974, and the Lenin Peace Prize in 1977. He was President of UNESCO's International Commission for the Study of Communication Problems 1977–80.

Mina M. Ramirez (PhD) is President of the Asian Social Institute, Manila, and Lecturer on the Sociology of the Filipino Family. She has written many papers and articles on Filipino family life and values. She is the author of *Understanding Philippine Social Realities through the Filipino Family* (1984).

Usha Vysasulu Reddi is head of the Department of Communication and Journalism, Osmania University, Hyderabad, India. She was Research Fellow at the East-West Centre, Honolulu, in 1982. She is the author of *The United Nations in China's Foreign Policy* and numerous articles on communication technology, policy and mass media news. She is currently working on a study for the International Communication and Youth Consortium.

Herbert I. Schiller is Professor of Communications at the University of California, San Diego. He is vice-president of the International Association for Mass Communication Research and a trustee of the International Institute of Communications. His many publications include *Mass Communications and American Empire* (1969), *Communication and Cultural Domination* (1976), *Who Knows: Information in the Age of the Fortune 500* (1981) and *Information and the Crisis Economy* (1984).

Michael Traber studied at Fordham University, and at New York University (PhD in Mass Communication). He was director of Mambo Press, Zimbabwe, 1962–70, director of Imba Press, Fribourg, Switzerland, 1970–72, and Senior Lecturer in Journalism at the Africa Literature Centre, Kitwe, Zambia, 1973–76. He is the author of *Rassismus und weisse Vorherrschaft* (1972) and *Das revolutionäre Afrika* (1972). He is currently on the staff of the World Association for Christian Communication, London.

Moema Viezzer is a teacher and social researcher living in São Paulo, Brazil. After working for many years in children's education, she dedicated herself to adult education in the rural areas of north-east Brazil. She is the author of *Si me permitan hablar* (1977), the testimony of a woman from the mines of Bolivia. At present she coordinates the work of Rede Mulher in Brazil.

Index